Bean Banquets
from Boston to Bombay

200 International, High-Fiber, Vegetarian Recipes

By
Patricia R. Gregory

Illustrations by Robert G. Gregory

Woodbridge Press / Santa Barbara, California

1992

Published and distributed by
Woodbridge Press Publishing Company
Post Office Box 6189
Santa Barbara, California 93160

Distributed simultaneously in the United States and Canada
Printed in the United States of America
Library of Congress Cataloging in Publication Data
Gregory, Patricia R.
  Bean banquets, from Boston to Bombay.
  Includes index.
  1. Cookery (Beans)   2. Cookery (Peas)   3. Cookery (Lentils)   4. Cookery, International.   I. Title.
TX803.B4G74   1984   641.6'565   84-3668
ISBN 0-88007-139-7

Bean Banquets
from Boston to Bombay

Contents

To my mother
and
Rob, Theresa, and Robert

Foreword: A Doctor's Prescription

PAT GREGORY HAS HAD THE GOOD FORTUNE of traveling throughout the world. She has worked with her husband, Dr. Robert Gregory, a much published historian, and has combined her own interests in the peoples, cultures, and foods in all the many parts of the world in which they traveled with an amazing sense of history. This has resulted in a marvelous repertoire of recipes to please the gourmet and gourmand alike.

I have been a devoted fan of hers for many years, and a dinner invitation from the Gregorys is always received with pleasant anticipation and wondering what the fare will be. Will it be Indian, Ethiopian, Middle Eastern, French, or Italian? Or will it possibly be a New England boiled dinner? Whatever, it is always a delight to the palate. When Pat asked me to write a foreword for her cookbook, I could hardly wait to see it. You can imagine my surprise when I received a manuscript devoted to the culinary glorification of the "lowly bean." Now that I have tried some of the recipes, I can only say, she's done it again. I love it!

Man's ability to find ways of transforming what is available within the limitations of economics and geography into gastronomical masterpieces has been a source of fascination for me for many years. The most interesting foods seem to come from the peasants' ability to take the leaves, seeds, roots, or meats available to them and cook, dry, salt, soak, and season them to tasty, nutritious sustenance.

The study of ecology demonstrates the distribution of animal life on our planet is largely dependent on the availability of food, particularly plant life. The climate, altitude, longitude, latitude, and air and sea currents determine plant distribution. This is responsible for the distribution of herbivores, which in turn, attract carnivores. Man, however, being omnivorous, was able to adjust his diet to the foods available in his region.

The versatility and ubiquity of the legume is demonstrated in this cookbook. The ease of growing legumes and the resultant availability have put peoples' imaginations throughout the world to the test.

Reading this book conjures up visions of peasant families enjoying the fruits of their labors and amply demonstrates the ability of people worldwide to take an abundant food source, the bean, and use it as a tasty, nutritious, and economical food.

Pat also points out that beans are a good source of protein, complex carbohydrates, trace minerals, and fiber. As a practicing surgeon, I am most interested in fiber and its attendant virtues. First, we must agree on a definition of fiber. The most popular definition is that fiber is the part of our food not digested by enzymes contained within the gastrointestinal tract, and therefore not absorbed. The fiber remains essentially unchanged and thus provides the bulk necessary for good bowel function.

Today, we routinely process the fiber out of our food, and we suffer a seemingly endless list of gastrointestinal and metabolic diseases. Many of these diseases have been linked to the consumption of fiber-depleted foods. The observations of Dennis Burkett on the absence of diseases such as constipation, hemorrhoids, diverticulitis, diverticulosis, and large bowel cancer in peoples in the less developed countries subsisting on a diet of totally unrefined foods led him to hypothesize that a diet that causes small concentrated stools increases the risks of polyps and colon cancer. Thomas Cleave, a British naval physician, hypothesized that it is not a low-fiber diet that harms us, but the intake of fiber-depleted refined foods. In other words, if our food were natural and unrefined, whatever our appetites told us to eat would provide us with whatever fiber we need. Their theories and hypotheses have been tested and challenged by the international medical profession and most agree that they are probably each right in many respects.

People who choose a fiber-rich unrefined diet reduce their chances of developing diseases of over-nutrition such as obesity, diabetes, gallstones, and coronary artery disease, the maladies of the mouth such as caries and periodontal disease, and diseases of the underworked colon such as constipation, hemorrhoids, diverticulosis, diverticulitis, appendicitis, and colon cancer. It is even hypothesized that the incidence of hiatal hernia may be reduced by such a diet.

The legumes, as Pat suggests, provide a good source of fiber, protein, carbohydrates, and some trace minerals, but they lack fats and particularly the essential fatty acid linoleic acid. One must also be aware that in a totally vegetarian diet, it is essential to take care to insure the adequate intake of all of the essential amino acids: methionine, threonine, tryptophan, isoleucine, leucine, lysine, valine, and phenylalanine. Pat has carefully pointed out these hazards in her introduction and has also diligently included fats, dairy products, and eggs in most of her recipes.

I am most pleased to prescribe the addition of legumes to a well-rounded diet. At any rate, happy eating to all gourmet and gourmand.

Fred W. Rio, M.D.

Acknowledgments

My MOST SINCERE THANKS to all of you who have contributed to this project, each in your own unique way.

Sue Bartley, Washington, DC
Shireen Carberry, Macon, IL
Lakshmi Crane, Syracuse, NY
Mr. V. G. Dave, Nairobi, Kenya
Rosemary Dewhirst, Houston, TX
Grace Flusche, Syracuse, NY
Barbara Gregory, Beverly Hills, CA
Ruth Gregory, Manhattan Beach, CA
Margaret Keats, Syracuse, NY
Nancy Kwok, Honolulu, HI
Joyce Levy, Cazenovia, NY
Flo Lewis, Syracuse, NY
Paul and Lainey Marsh, Scarborough, Ont., Canada
Toshie Mori, Tokyo, Japan
Dick Morris, Honolulu, HI
Anne Muller, Strasbourg, France
Nyambura Mwangi, Nakuru, Kenya
Merun Nasser, Boulder, CO
Anthoula Natsoulas, Dayton, OH
Mrs. Pushkar Oza, Bombay, India
Hansa Pandya, Rajkot, India
Carmelle Pietrantoni, Syracuse, NY
Lisa Pollard, Shepton Mallet, England
Mona El Bayadi Racine, Boston, MA
Don Raleigh, Honolulu, HI
Bob Rayback, Syracuse, NY
Fred and Charlene Rio, Granada Hills, CA

Theresa Rio, Granada Hills, CA
Barbara Scruggs, Syracuse, NY
Dana Seidenberg, Washington, DC
Nancy Sharp, Syracuse, NY
Mort and Nancy Sogaard, Palos Verdes, CA
Terri Sopher, Syracuse, NY
Noor and Shirin Velji, Bethesda, MD
Beryl Wade, Honolulu, HI
Paulette Wamego, editor, Santa Barbara, CA
Nanda Weeks, Syracuse, NY
Marguerite Yearns, Winston-Salem, NC
Ebikake Yeri-Obidake, Oproza, Nigeria
Arafa Zehra, Lahore, Pakistan

BENEFITS OF BEANS

Introduction

Benefits of Beans

DRIED LEGUMES HAVE A NEW IMAGE. They have glamour. The reason for this is that everyone, rich and poor, young and old, is interested in good health. People are walking, running, jogging, doing aerobic dance, swimming, and playing tennis, racquetball, and squash. But most of all, they are changing their eating habits. They are eating less meat and saturated fats and are adding whole grains, beans, and other high-fiber foods to their diet.

Dried legumes, that is beans, lentils, peas, and chickpeas (garbanzos), are slimming, healthful, unadulterated, readily available, easily prepared, and can be really flavorful. They are the last high-protein food that is still economical.

A high-fiber, high-carbohydrate diet helps one to reduce excess weight. Such a diet has few calories and contains foods that are filling and satisfying. Beans are high in fiber and carbohydrates, and they contain no fat. One-half cup of home-baked beans contains only about 150 calories, and one-half cup of cooked kidney beans has about 100 calories, approximately the same as a large apple or orange. By comparison, one small (4-ounce) slice of sirloin or tenderloin steak contains about 285 calories.

Let's consider what might be an average day's menu. If, for example, a person had for breakfast a bowl of oatmeal (¾ cup—100 calories) with one-half cup of skim milk (40 calories) and two teaspoons of brown sugar (30 calories), and a half grapefruit (50 calories), he would have consumed about 220 calories.

If for lunch he had one cup of split pea soup (165

13

calories), two slices of whole wheat bread (120 calories), one large glass of skim milk (80 calories), and one large apple (100 calories), he would have had only about 465 calories.

At dinner time, when one usually eats more, if he ate one cup of a bean preparation of his choice (250 to 350 calories), one and one-half cups of cooked brown or white rice (200 calories), one and one-half cups of broccoli with one-half tablespoon of butter (114 calories), one large stalk of celery (6 calories), one-half medium cantaloupe (50 calories), and one large glass of skim milk (80 calories), his intake would total 700 to 800 calories. By day's end, this person would have eaten three satisfying, nutritious, high-fiber meals and would have consumed only about 1385 to 1485 calories. Besides, he would not have felt hungry between meals. Most people could add another 100 to 150 calories and still lose weight.

By combining dried legumes with grains such as rice, wheat, barley, corn, and oats, and/or eggs, dairy products, some nuts and seeds, a perfectly adequate, high-quality, protein diet can be achieved. (It is essential that legumes and these complementary foods be eaten at the same meal, since our bodies do not store proteins.)

As we all know, proteins are essential to the human body, which is made up mostly of protein—in fact, hundreds of different kinds of proteins. It is necessary, therefore, to follow daily a diet containing sufficient and complete proteins to ensure the growth and maintenance of body tissues. In addition to building and renewing body cells, protein helps regulate the acid-base balance of the body, aids the formation of body hormones and enzymes, and promotes resistance to disease.

Proteins are composed of twenty amino acids, and nine of these are termed "essential." Because the body cannot synthesize them, they must be supplied by the food we eat. The nine essential amino acids—isoleucine, leucine, lysine, threonine, tryptophan, methionine, phenylalanine, valine, and histidine (for children)—are needed simultaneously in order for our bodies to carry out vital

14

protein synthesis. The remaining amino acids, known as "inessential," are equally important, but they can be manufactured by the human body if it has adequate nitrogen, which is provided generally in food.

The plant foods richest in proteins are dried legumes (with soybeans having the highest protein quality). Whether we receive the bulk of our protein from combined legumes and grains or from meat, we must keep in mind the importance of eating other foods along with these. Raw and cooked vegetables and fruits, some eggs, and dairy products should be consumed to ensure a well-balanced diet that includes all the essential nutrients. This is the key to a healthful diet.

Besides being rich in protein, dried legumes are a vital source of the B vitamins, especially riboflavin, niacin, and vitamin B6. They contain minerals such as calcium, iron, and potassium, and are low in sodium. Their high-fiber content is an excellent aid to digestion. Leading scientists claim that the lack of fiber in our diet may be the cause of some types of cancer, especially of the colon and rectum. Researchers also are finding evidence suggesting that protease inhibitors found in beans may play a role in preventing tumor development. Other diseases that eating beans seems to help prevent are heart disease, gallbladder disease, and diabetes.

Research has shown that a high-fiber, high-carbohydrate diet lowers levels of triglycerides and cholesterol, which may help prevent the development of clogged arteries and heart disease. This is especially important to diabetics because clogged arteries and heart disease are complications of diabetes and are the causes of about three-fourths of the deaths among diabetics. Triglycerides and cholesterol are fatty substances in the blood, and high levels of them are thought to be a factor in both heart and gallbladder disease. The types of dietary fiber researchers have found most effective in lowering cholesterol levels in the blood are the soluble fibers, gums, pectins, and mucilages, all found in dried beans, peas, and lentils, some fruits, and oats.

15

Other recent research shows a remarkable correlation between consumption of beans and rapid and slow rises in blood sugar and blood insulin. For many years diabetologists and nutritionists believed that simple carbohydrates such as sugars, like glucose, sucrose, and fructose, caused a sudden rise in blood sugar, while complex carbohydrates, which are the starches found in potatoes, corn, wheat, and rice, resulted in a slower rise in blood sugar and blood insulin. It now has been discovered that this is not true. Rather, individual foods of both simple and complex carbohydrates vary in their influence on blood sugar. Researchers have found that although sweet potatoes and rice have little effect on blood glucose, white potatoes cause the blood sugar to soar. The glucose responses rose, in increasing order, with rice, bread, corn, and potatoes. However, pasta produced much lower blood glucose rises than any of these. Moreover, dried legumes turned out to be really outstanding in that blood glucose rose only about half as much as with the cereals. It seems that pasta and beans constitutes the most ideal combination. It has been suggested that people develop diabetes in adulthood because they eat the kind of carbohydrates that produce rapid rises in blood sugar rather than because they have eaten too many carbohydrates.

Although health is the foremost reason to incorporate more legumes into our diet, we cannot overlook the ecological and economic advantages of eating legumes. Human population has been expanding at an enormous rate while agricultural land has been giving way to urban sprawl. As this continues, it is expected by some that within the next two decades food shortage will become the world's greatest crisis. It is said that an acre in soybeans will supply enough protein to last a person for over six years; an acre in wheat, rice, or corn will keep a person for two to two and a half years; an acre in poultry will keep him for only six months; an acre in beef will keep him for only two months.

Beans are not only easy to grow and prolific bearers of nutritious food, but they are unique in that they can take

16

life-giving nitrogen from the air and fix it in the soil through their roots which contain certain nitrogen fixing bacteria. This process produces the high protein content in legumes and also improves the fertility of the soil.

The economic advantage of eating beans is obvious. During the past few years when the cost of food generally has soared, the price of beans has remained stable. One can still buy a pound of beans, enough for a family of six, for well under one dollar.

Legumes have been popular in North America, but they have not been the principal source of protein as they have for most peoples in the world. In Europe they are eaten far more. Raised in an Italian family in the United States, I was fortunate to have legumes as a vital part of my diet since childhood. My mother continues to produce her wonderful bean dishes, to our delight. Europeans generally cook with legumes to a much greater extent than we do, although their dishes, such as the French cassoulet, usually include meat. But even in Europe, beans are not eaten so much as they are in other parts of the world. In East Asia, high-protein soybeans are used extensively, mostly in the forms of bean curd (doufu or tofu), miso, and tamari (naturally fermented soy sauce). These soybean products can be found in most of our grocery stores. Bean curd, which is made from soybean milk, is used throughout East Asia, and miso, a fermented soybean paste, is used as a soup base and a seasoning mainly in Japan. I have included a few of my favorite recipes using these ingredients even though they are by-products of beans and not the beans themselves.

Dal (dried peas and lentils) and chick-peas are the legumes most commonly eaten in India. The Indians, like the British and others, call their legumes "pulses." When we lived in India, we were delighted with the well-balanced, tasty diet to which we were introduced. In this mostly vegetarian country, people tend to eat a combination of one or two of the many pulses, accompanied by rice and chapatis (flat, round, unleavened, whole wheat bread, much like the Mexican tortillas), yoghurt, and raw

17

and cooked vegetables. Pickles and chutneys are also included in this exciting, spicy diet of contrasting and complementary foods.

Complementary beans and corn are favorite foods in Mexico, while in South and Central America the delicious black beans are consumed by all.

Throughout the Middle East and North Africa, beans are eaten daily by the majority of the people. Fava beans cook all night in large copper pots in Cairo. Before dawn they are delivered to the many hotels and restaurants in the city. The *ful mudamas* is ladled into small containers for thousands who are having it for the morning repast. It is sometimes taken with an egg, but mostly it is eaten simply with a little olive oil and lemon juice and with the freshly baked, flat, round pita bread.

In the United States, too, beans have been consumed widely. Red beans, pinto beans, and black-eyed peas are frequently eaten in the southern states, while in the North, especially in Michigan, navy beans and great northern beans are more often found. Boston claims the best baked beans in the world, and in the West, red kidney beans and pinto beans vie for top place for making hot and spicy chili.

Contrary to popular opinion, legumes can be prepared in such a way that they will cause little or no digestive disturbance. It is true that many of the bean preparations that we know can cause flatulence. When told that they should eat more legumes, some people reply that they cannot eat beans or that they dare eat them only rarely. But the problem is really one of preparation. I have tested my mother's cooking technique on my family and friends, and all agree that they had no difficulty after eating my bean dishes. The body does, however, need to adjust to digesting a high-fiber diet when it is not used to it, and during that short period of adjustment, some minor disturbance may occur.

Meat has not been included in the recipes in this book, not even in small quantities, even though the favorite bean dishes in the Western world almost always include

18

some meat. One reason is that animal foods of any kind—pork, beef, chicken, even fish—tend to contain saturated fats and contaminants harmful to man. Another is that legumes prepared without meat can be very tasty and deserve to be enjoyed in their own right.

Dried legumes are among the least processed items in the supermarket. They are not subjected to preservatives or other chemicals generally used in processing foods, and they have not been given drugs or hormones. Also, beans are protected by pods and, therefore, have lower residues than meat. They are about the only food left in the supermarket where a little bit of earth may still be found.

The benefits of beans have been recognized since man first began to cultivate his foods. Beans go back to the cradle of civilization, about 8000 B.C., in the Middle East, and to about 6000 B.C. in the high altitudes of Peru. In China soybeans were cultivated earlier than 3000 B.C. From these early beginnings, legumes spread all over the world. They were popular in ancient Greece and Rome and, in fact, were used for counting votes in elections held in ancient Rome. It is no wonder that peoples from so many parts of the world still rely on beans as a principal source of protein, are so knowledgeable about the benefits of eating grains and other complementary protein foods with their legumes, and have developed so many tasty ways of preparing beans.

With many of the recipes, I offer a number of suggestions for combinations, and other serving ideas. Most of the recipes are easily prepared, and when there is little time, even canned legumes may be used. It is not necessary to eat meat even if you do not care to eat legumes every day. Eggs or dairy products offer a nutritious change of pace. But the various legume dishes will provide great variety, are delicious and substantial, beneficial to weight control, satisfy good nutrition standards, and ease the strain on the budget.

Buying & Storing Dried Legumes

Buying and Storing Dried Legumes

Almost all grocery stores sell some varieties of dried legumes. Usually red kidney beans, pinto beans, baby and large lima beans, navy or pea beans, great northern beans, yellow and green split peas, and lentils can be easily found. Many grocery stores have expanded their selections, and one can often find dried chick-peas, black beans, red beans, pink beans, Roman or cranberry beans, marrow beans, black-eyed peas, and others. Nearly all grocers also stock canned legumes.

Some stores have a special section devoted to Oriental foods, where adzuki beans, fava beans, mung beans, bean curd (tofu or doufu), and even some Indian dals can be found. There are also Oriental shops that carry a complete line of pulses, grains, and spices. If there is not one in your area, you can order ingredients by mail.

Food cooperatives and health food stores usually have a wide selection of dried legumes such as soybeans, mung beans, chick-peas, and lentils. Bean curd and miso are frequently available too. By shopping around, you can find all the ingredients cited in this book.

Beans are easily stored and will keep almost indefinitely. However, those kept more than a year will take a long time to cook, so it is a good idea to rotate your supply. Beans and lentils keep best in airtight containers. They look so attractive with their warm, earthy colors that you may want to display them in glass jars in your kitchen.

Cooked legumes will last in the refrigerator four to five days, but they can be frozen and kept for up to six months. Do not add salt or other ingredients to cooked beans that you plan to store in the refrigerator or freezer—they will be more digestible. To thaw frozen legumes, just place containers in hot water. Beans also can be thawed quickly in a microwave oven.

21

Mail order sources are as follows:

Bezjian Grocery
4725 Santa Monica Blvd.
Los Angeles, CA 90029

Haig's Delicacies
642 Clement St.
San Francisco, CA 94118

Antone's
Box 3352
Houston, TX 77001

International House of Foods
440 W. Gorham St.
Madison, WI 53703

Kalustyan Orient Export Trading Corp.
123 Lexington Ave.
New York, NY 10016

Spices and Foods Unlimited, Inc.
2018 A. Florida Ave., N.W.
Washington, DC 20009

Cambridge Coffee, Tea and Spice House
1765 Massachusetts Ave.
Cambridge, MA 02138

S. Enkin Incorporated
1201 St. Lawrence St.
Montreal 129, Quebec

PREPARING THE BANQUET
Cooking Legumes

Preparing the Banquet: Cooking Legumes

This simple method of cooking legumes takes a minimum of time and eliminates digestive problems some people have after eating beans.

In a large saucepan, rinse and drain legumes which have been picked over to remove any bits of dirt, stones, or imperfect beans. Add about triple their volume of cold water (about seven cups water to one pound beans). I usually put my index finger in the water to the top of the legumes. When the water reaches my second knuckle, I know there is enough. Use more water for soybeans because they absorb more.

Bring the water to a full, rolling boil, and cook the legumes for one minute. Skim the foam while the beans are boiling. Cover the pan, remove it from the heat, and let the legumes stand for two hours or longer (at least one hour). Be careful with soybeans since they ferment easily. You may refrigerate them to avoid this.

After the soaking period, beans may be drained and fresh water added. This will help prevent flatulence associated with eating legumes. Those who are not sensitive to digestive problems should cook their beans in the soaking water, as it contains vitamins and minerals.

When cooking legumes, bring the soaked legumes to a slow boil and allow legumes to cook slowly until they are at the desired softness. Cook them softer for soups and other dishes and firmer for salads. While they are gently boiling, prepare the other ingredients for the bean dish, as well as the remainder of the meal.

It is important not to add to the legumes any salt, flavorings, or other ingredients until shortly before serving them. Withholding seasonings until the last possible moment, soaking for at least an hour, and changing to fresh cooking water are the key factors in eliminating digestive problems. For those who are extremely sensitive to this problem, beans may be rinsed at the end of the cooking period and water may be substituted for recipes requiring bean broth.

Timing legumes for cooking is difficult because so much depends on their age, how long they have soaked, and how soft you want them. The fresher they are the less time they take to cook. After brown lentils have soaked, they will be cooked sufficiently for salads within only one or two minutes, while another two or three minutes is desirable for soups. Indian dals and split peas, after soaking, usually take about twenty to thirty minutes to cook, except for channa dal, which can take one to one and a half hours. Most beans that have soaked will take between thirty-five minutes and one hour to cook. Baby limas and black-eyed peas can take about thirty-five minutes, great northern beans, large limas, and pinto beans about forty minutes, kidney beans and navy or pea beans about forty-five minutes, and black beans about one hour. Chick-peas can take one and a half to three hours, and fava beans and soybeans three to four hours. I recommend buying skinned fava which take less than one hour to cook.

A pressure cooker can be a time and energy saver. Pressure cooking is not recommended for lentils, including most dals and split peas, which cook so quickly anyway, or for black beans, limas, or other beans that foam a lot and thus can cause the vent in the cooker to become clogged by a bean skin. But for most beans, especially soybeans, chick-peas, and fava beans, a pressure cooker can be very useful if used with care. Cooking times vary greatly but most beans will take about ten to fifteen minutes under fifteen pounds pressure. Chick-peas will take fifteen to twenty minutes, and soybeans and fava beans can take thirty to forty-five minutes. If beans have not soaked, add five to ten minutes.

When using the pressure cooker, change the water before cooking the beans, and use four times as much water as beans. Skim the water before bringing them up to pressure, add 1 tablespoon of oil to help control foaming (this is especially important with soybeans, which tend to foam a lot), and do not fill the cooker more than two-thirds full.

I do not recommend a slow cooker for bean cooking because a high temperature should be reached, especially for red kidney beans. They contain insignificant amounts of toxic substances (hemagglutinins) which are eliminated through boiling.

Bean cooking can easily be fitted into a busy schedule. If you plan to cook legumes for dinner, bring them to a rapid boil for one minute in the morning and let them soak most of the day. Then cook them while you prepare the rest of the meal. If you plan to have them for breakfast, you can cook them the day before and then add the flavoring in the morning. For lunch, let them soak overnight and cook them in the morning. Again, flavorings should be added only shortly before serving.

To outline the cooking process:

1. Pick over the legumes and rinse.
2. Add triple their volume of cold water.
3. Boil one minute, cover pan, and remove from heat.
4. Allow to stand for two hours or longer.
5. If desired, drain legumes and add fresh water.
6. Boil gently or pressure cook until done.

hors-d'œuvres

Hors d'oeuvres

Salt and other flavorings may be added to chick-peas before baking, but I prefer them plain.

Chick-Pea Nuts

chick-peas
melted butter

1. Cook chick-peas until tender (see pages 23–26). Drain.

2. Place cooked chick-peas on a baking sheet in a single layer. Add a little melted butter and shake pan to help coat chick-peas.

3. Bake in 350°F. oven for 1 hour and 15 minutes or until chick-peas are golden brown and crisp. When completely cool, store in an airtight container.

This savory Indian snack is nice to have on hand. It is enjoyed at any time, but in India it is especially appreciated with afternoon tea. We might call this "nuts and bolts."

Chevra

(Indian Snacks)

½ cup channa dal
Soaking liquid:
   1 cup water
   ½ cup milk
Noodle mixture:
   4 cups chick-pea flour (also called gram flour or besan)
   2½ teaspoons salt
   2½ teaspoons turmeric
   ¼ teaspoon asafetida (hing)
   1½ teaspoons ajawan seeds, pulverized with mortar and pestle
   (optional)
   ½ cup peanut oil
   4 tablespoons lemon juice
   water to make 1¾ cups liquid ingredients
1 cup flaked rice (phoa)
2 cups puffed rice
3 cups oil for frying
1 cup raw peanuts
1 cup raw cashew nuts
½ teaspoon ground coriander
½ teaspoon ground cumin
½ teaspoon granulated fructose sugar
½ teaspoon cayenne
½ cup golden raisins

1. Wash the dal in cold water, drain and put in saucepan with soaking liquid. Soak overnight or bring to a rolling boil and let boil for 1 minute. Cover pan, remove from heat, and soak dal for 2 hours. Drain and set on paper towels to dry. The dal needs to be thoroughly dried for frying or the oil may bubble over. The dal can be oven dried for a few minutes if necessary.

2. Combine the chick-pea flour, 2 teaspoons of the salt, 2 teaspoons of the turmeric, the asafetida, and the pulverized ajawan seeds in a bowl. In a 2-cup measuring cup, combine the peanut oil, lemon juice, and enough water to make 1¾ cups liquid. Stir and add this to the dry ingre-

dients. Mix thoroughly to make a smooth batter. It is now ready to be deep-fried. Set aside.

3. Lightly brown the flaked rice and the puffed rice in a moderate oven, about 350°F. Place rice in a large mixing bowl.

4. Heat the oil for frying in an Indian karhai, a wok, a deep-fryer, or a saucepan to a temperature of about 375°F.

5. Push some of the chick-pea flour batter through the holes of a ricer or through a colander into the hot oil. Fry these noodles 1 or 2 minutes or until they are golden brown. Transfer them to paper towels to drain. Fry the remaining noodles in a similar manner. When they are all fried and drained, place them in the bowl with the flaked and puffed rice.

6. Fry the peanuts and cashews. When they are lightly browned, drain them and put them in the bowl with the noodles and rice.

7. When the dal is completely dry, fry for less than 1 minute. Drain and add to the bowl.

8. This mixture will nearly fill the mixing bowl. Sprinkle the remaining ½ teaspoon salt, ½ teaspoon turmeric, the coriander, cumin, sugar, and cayenne over the chevra. Add raisins and mix well.

Chevra will keep in airtight containers for several weeks.

These pakoras with the accompanying chutney dip are spicy, really delicious, and very popular.

Pakora

(A Deep-Fried Hors d'oeuvre or Snack from India)

1 cup chick-pea flour (also called gram flour and besan)
½ teaspoon salt
¼ to ½ teaspoon cayenne
½ teaspoon ajway or ajawan seeds (optional)
1 or 2 small hot green peppers, finely chopped
1½ tablespoons finely minced fresh ginger
½ to ⅔ cup water
slices or pieces of onion, potato, cauliflower, zucchini, or other
    vegetables
oil for deep-frying

1. Make a thick batter using all ingredients except vegetable pieces and frying oil. Beat briskly with a whisk to remove any lumps. Should be similar to a pancake batter.

2. Heat about 1½ inches of oil in an Indian karhai, a wok, or a deep-fryer to a medium-hot temperature, about 350°F. Dip vegetable pieces in batter and fry, a few at a time, in the hot oil. Turn to brown both sides. Drain on paper towels and serve hot as an appetizer or as a snack with yoghurt chutney. Makes about 30.

Yoghurt Chutney

(An Indian Dipping Sauce)

1 cup plain yoghurt
1 tablespoon fresh mint leaves
¼ teaspoon salt
¼ teaspoon ground cumin
dash cayenne

1. Put into blender 1 rounded tablespoon of the yoghurt, mint leaves, salt, cumin, and cayenne. Blend 30 seconds.

2. Drain remaining yoghurt, if necessary, and combine with blended mixture in a small bowl. Serve with pakoras.

In Tanzania, African vendors prepare and sell these delicious snacks on the street. They place about four or five of the bhajias on skewers as they are fried and sell them to passersby. The bhajias make fantastic hors d'oeuvres, may be served as a first course with dinner, are enjoyed with afternoon tea, or as a snack anytime.

Tanzanian Bhajias

(Deep-Fried, Spicy Bean Balls)

½ pound whole mung beans
2 cloves garlic, chopped
½ cup water
1 rounded teaspoon ground coriander
½ to 1 teaspoon cayenne
1 hot green chili pepper or jalapeño, finely chopped
½ green pepper, finely chopped
2 medium onions, chopped
¼ cup chopped fresh coriander
salt
oil for deep-frying

1. Soak mung beans in water overnight. Drain.
2. Put through blender with garlic and water, in batches. Use only enough water to facilitate blending—½ cup should be sufficient. Batter need not be smooth.
3. Pour bean mixture into a bowl and combine with remaining ingredients, except oil.
4. Heat oil to 350°F. Drop mixture from a teaspoon into hot oil, or use a cocktail meatballer to form balls. Fry a few at a time until they are well browned. If they do not hold together, pour bean mixture into a large strainer or colander and let some of the liquid drain out.
5. When bhajias are fried, drain on paper towels. Makes about 3 dozen. Serve hot with coconut chutney.

Coconut Chutney

(A Dipping Sauce from Tanzania)

1 cup grated unsweetened coconut
⅓ to ½ cup water, if using fresh coconut (¾ cup water if using dried)
⅓ cup lemon juice
1 cup fresh coriander leaves
2 to 4 hot green peppers, seeded and chopped (1 teaspoon cayenne
    may be substituted)

1. Put all ingredients through blender.
2. Pour into small serving bowl and garnish with a few coriander leaves or with a light sprinkling of paprika. Serve with Tanzanian bhajias.

Good, hot hors d'oeuvre!

Bean Ball Surprises

¾ pound dried navy or pea beans
1 egg, beaten
½ onion, finely chopped
¼ cup whole wheat flour
2 tablespoons minced fresh parsley
¼ teaspoon oregano
salt
⅛ teaspoon white pepper
cheddar, Swiss, Monterey Jack, or your favorite cheese
oil for deep-frying

1. Cook beans according to basic directions (see pages 23–26). Drain.
2. Mash beans and combine with egg, onion, flour, parsley, oregano, salt, and pepper.
3. Cut cheese in small cubes. Surround a cheese cube with about 2 teaspoons of bean mixture. Form into ball, completely enclosing cheese. Repeat with remaining bean mixture and cheese cubes.
4. Heat oil in a deep saucepan or deep-fryer to about 375°F. Fry a few balls at a time for 3 or 4 minutes or until

golden brown. If they disintegrate when frying, dip them in beaten egg before frying. Drain on paper towels. Serve immediately. Makes approximately 3 dozen.

Serve with a French mustard.

In the South, it is believed that if you eat black-eyed peas on January 1, you will have good luck all year. The symbolism of good luck from black-eyed peas is an old tradition that comes from West Africa.

Texas Caviar

½ pound dried black-eyed peas
2 tablespoons peanut oil
1 large onion, chopped
1 large green pepper, chopped
1 jalapeño pepper, seeded and finely chopped
3 bay leaves
2 cloves garlic, crushed
¼ cup peanut oil
2 tablespoons wine vinegar
2 tablespoons chopped fresh parsley
salt
⅛ teaspoon cayenne

1. Cook beans according to basic directions (see pages 23–26). Drain well.

2. Heat 2 tablespoons peanut oil in a frying pan and sauté onion, green pepper, jalapeño pepper, bay leaves, and garlic until vegetables are soft but not browned.

3. In a bowl, combine beans with contents of frying pan. Remove bay leaves.

4. Add ¼ cup peanut oil, wine vinegar, parsley, salt, and cayenne. Toss the caviar thoroughly but gently.

Serve as appetizer or side dish with lightly toasted whole wheat bread squares, warmed pita bread, or crackers.

These popular treats disappear as quickly as you can make them.

Mexican Nachos

tortilla chips (see recipe page 36)
frijoles (see recipe page 157)
1 small jar pickled jalapeño peppers, sliced
sliced sharp cheddar cheese

1. Place tortilla chips on a baking sheet.
2. Top each tortilla chip with frijoles, a slice of jalapeño pepper, and a slice of cheese.
3. Place under broiler for 2 or 3 minutes, or until cheese melts. Serve immediately.

This hot, tasty dip is always popular at parties. I have had many requests for the recipe.

Mexican Bean Dip

½ recipe frijoles
½ teaspoon chili powder
1 3-ounce can chopped green chilies
1 cup grated sharp cheddar cheese
2 tablespoons chopped green onions
½ cup fresh tomatoes, peeled and chopped
few drops hot pepper sauce, if desired

1. Prepare frijoles according to recipe on page 157. Combine frijoles with chili powder and canned chilies.
2. Pour frijoles into an attractive pottery bowl. Place in 350°F. preheated oven until very hot. Remove from oven, sprinkle with cheese, and return to oven for 5 minutes to melt cheese.
3. Remove from oven and sprinkle with green onions and tomatoes. Add a few drops of hot pepper sauce if desired.
Serve with tortilla chips.

Tortilla Chips

corn tortillas
oil for frying
salt, if desired

1. Cut tortillas in wedges (8 wedges per tortilla).
2. Heat ½ inch of oil in skillet. When hot, fry tortilla wedges, a few at a time, until crisp and lightly browned.
3. Remove and drain on paper towels. Salt lightly if desired.

This popular dip with its colorful and tasty layers is as appealing to see as it is to eat.

Seven Layer California Dip

1 16-ounce can refried beans or 1 recipe frijoles (page 157)
1 3-ounce can chopped chilies
1 large, ripe avocado
1 tablespoon chopped green onions
2 teaspoons lemon juice
¼ teaspoon salt
½ cup sour cream
½ cup hot taco sauce
1½ cups grated cheddar cheese
½ cup chopped ripe olives
1 chopped tomato
tortilla chips (see recipe above)

1. Combine refried beans with chilies and spread on a round, 10-inch platter to 1 inch from the edge.
2. Prepare guacamole by mashing avocado and combining it with green onions, lemon juice, and salt. Spread guacamole over refried beans.
3. Carefully spread sour cream over guacamole and top with taco sauce.
4. Sprinkle evenly with cheddar cheese, olives, and tomato.
5. Serve with tortilla chips. Place some of the chips at-

tractively around the edge of the dip and put those remaining in a separate bowl. Serves 6 or more.

For a large party, double recipe and assemble dip in a shallow, glass dish, approximately 8 x 12 inches. Layer the refried bean mixture, guacamole, taco sauce, and cheddar cheese. Top with sour cream. Make 2-inch stripes of chopped olives and tomatoes running the length of the dish with stripes of sour cream showing between the olives and tomatoes. The black, red, and white stripes make an attractive dip.

This irresistible paté makes an elegant hors d'oeuvre.

Haricot Blanc Paté

½ cup dried great northern beans (1½ cups cooked)
1 tablespoon Dijon-style mustard
1 clove garlic, crushed
2 tablespoons fresh lemon juice
¼ cup olive oil
salt
⅛ teaspoon white pepper
2 tablespoons well drained capers, plus a few for garnish
2 tablespoons finely chopped parsley
paprika

1. Cook beans according to basic directions (see pages 23–26). Drain well.

2. Place beans in blender jar with mustard, garlic, lemon juice, olive oil, salt, and pepper. Blend until smooth and creamy. Scrape sides of blender jar with rubber spatula. Blend 5 seconds longer.

3. Pour bean mixture into a small bowl and combine with capers and parsley. Pour onto serving dish. Garnish with paprika and a few capers.

Serve with whole wheat toasted bread squares, warmed pita bread, or crackers.

This old-time Arabic dip is becoming increasingly popular in the Western world.

Hummos bi Tahini

(Middle Eastern Chick-Pea Dip)

1 cup dried chick-peas
2 small cloves garlic
4 tablespoons tahini (sesame seed paste)
juice from 2 lemons (4 to 5 tablespoons lemon juice)
salt
dash white pepper
olive oil
fresh parsley
paprika

1. Cook chick-peas according to basic directions (see pages 23–26). Drain.

2. Place cooked and drained chick-peas, garlic, tahini, lemon juice, salt, and pepper in blender. Blend to make a thick puree. Add a little water if necessary to facilitate blending.

3. Pour puree into a shallow bowl or onto individual plates.

4. Make a swirl design on top and dribble a little olive oil over.

5. Garnish with parsley and a light sprinkling of paprika. Serve with whole wheat pita bread.

You may use leftover Moros y Cristianos, if you have any, for this dip, by mashing bean preparation, adding lemon juice, and topping it with chopped parsley and green onion, or you may use the following recipe.

Black Bean Dip

½ cup dried black beans
2 tablespoons butter
1 small onion, finely chopped
1 clove garlic, mashed
1 stalk celery, finely chopped
¼ teaspoon dried marjoram
¼ teaspoon ground cumin
1 tablespoon lemon juice (or to taste)
salt
hot pepper sauce
1 tablespoon mayonnaise
chopped parsley
chopped green onion

1. Cook beans according to basic directions until very soft (see pages 23–26). Drain, reserving very little of the broth.

2. In a skillet, melt butter and sauté onion, garlic, celery, marjoram, and cumin until vegetables are lightly browned. Add lemon juice and just enough bean broth to cook vegetables thoroughly. When vegetables are very well done, combine with the beans and add salt and hot pepper sauce. Cook 5 minutes.

3. Mash bean mixture but do not puree. Stir in mayonnaise and add more lemon juice and hot pepper sauce if desired.

4. Pour into a bowl and refrigerate or serve at room temperature. Before serving, sprinkle with parsley and green onion. This is good with crackers, toast squares, or pita bread.

There are many combinations that can be used to make a tasty dip with tofu. This one is my favorite.

Tofu Dip

5 or 6 ounces tofu
1 tablespoon apple cider vinegar
2 tablespoons olive oil
2 teaspoons tamari soy sauce
¼ teaspoon liquid fructose sugar
salt
¼ teaspoon white pepper
⅛ teaspoon ground ginger
2 tablespoons sliced green onions
1 tablespoon chopped chives for garnish

1. Blend all ingredients, except chives, until smooth.
2. Pour into an attractive bowl and chill.
3. Just before serving, top with chives.

Serve with strips of carrot, celery, zucchini, green pepper, cucumber, and with green onions and cauliflower pieces.

SOUPS

Soups

Good old American navy bean soup is sometimes called Senate soup because it is served daily in the lunchroom of the U.S. Senate.

Navy Bean Soup

½ pound dried navy or pea beans
2 tablespoons butter
1 onion, chopped
1 clove garlic, mashed
2 carrots (1 cup), chopped
1 stalk celery with a few leaves (1 cup), chopped
½ cup tomato puree
2 cups vegetable broth or bouillon
1 bay leaf
¼ teaspoon dried thyme
1 rounded tablespoon chopped fresh parsley
salt
⅛ teaspoon white pepper
¼ cup cream
½ cup milk

1. Cook beans according to basic directions (see pages 23–26), using 4 cups water, until very soft.

2. Melt butter over medium heat in a soup kettle. Sauté onion and garlic until onion is transparent.

3. Add the carrots, celery, tomato puree, broth, bay leaf, and thyme. Cook mixture until vegetables are very tender.

4. Shortly before serving, add beans with bean broth, parsley, salt, and pepper.

5. Bring soup to a boil. Add cream and milk and heat to boiling point, but do not boil. Serve immediately to 3 or 4.

I like to have this with whole wheat toast, sliced cheese, and sliced avocado.

This hearty chowder tastes especially good on a frosty evening.

Bean and Leek Chowder

¾ pound dried navy beans
3 tablespoons butter
1 medium onion, chopped
2 carrots, scraped, halved lengthwise, and sliced into half discs
1 pound (3 medium) potatoes, peeled and diced
1 pound leeks, sliced—include the tender portion of the green
2 cups water
1½ cups milk
salt
white pepper
2 tablespoons chopped fresh parsley

1. Cook beans according to basic directions (see pages 23–26). Reserve broth.

2. In a soup kettle, melt butter and sauté onion and carrots until onion is transparent. Add potatoes and leeks and sauté about 5 minutes more. The vegetables should not brown. Add the water and let simmer until vegetables are tender.

3. Add beans, bean broth, milk, salt, pepper, and parsley. Bring to a boil. Turn heat low and simmer for 5 minutes. Serves 4 to 6.

I serve whole wheat toast with this chowder, and I like to top off the meal with assorted cheeses and fresh fruit.

American Indians called squash, corn, and beans "Three Sisters" because they grew together, dependent on each other. The corn stalks support the climbing bean plants, the beans give nitrogen to the soil for its enrichment, and the squash grows low, large leaves to control weeds and hold the moisture in the ground.

Three Sisters Soup

½ pound dried baby lima beans
2 pounds peeled and cubed pumpkin
5 cups vegetable broth
1 onion, chopped
1 large leek, washed well and sliced
2 cups fresh or frozen corn kernels
1 cup light cream or half and half
salt
¼ teaspoon white pepper
chopped chives

1. Cook beans according to basic directions (see pages 23–26). Drain.

2. Place pumpkin, broth, onion, and leek in a kettle. Bring to a boil, reduce heat, and simmer until pumpkin is soft.

3. Puree vegetable mixture in a blender, in batches, and return to the kettle.

4. Add corn and beans, bring to a boil, reduce heat and simmer 5 minutes.

5. Add cream, salt, and pepper. When very hot, but not boiling, serve. Sprinkle with chives. Serves 4 to 6.

This hearty soup needs only a good, whole-grain bread and a salad to accompany it. Indian pudding with vanilla ice cream would be a fitting dessert.

These common red beans become a gourmet delight with this preparation.

Red Bean Soup

1 pound dried red beans
1 large onion, chopped
2 cloves garlic, mashed
2 tablespoons butter
1 cup chopped celery
1 cup chopped carrots
1 cup sliced mushrooms
2 bay leaves
¼ teaspoon thyme
¼ teaspoon marjoram
¼ teaspoon summer savory
½ cup apple juice
salt
⅛ teaspoon white pepper
1 hard-boiled egg, grated

1. Cook beans according to basic recipe directions (see pages 23–26), but increase water to 10 cups.

2. In a large skillet, sauté onion and garlic in butter until onion is transparent. Add celery, carrots, and mushrooms. Continue to sauté. Add herbs and juice. Simmer until vegetables are tender.

3. Do not drain beans, but mash some of them with a potato masher.

4. Combine vegetables with beans and add salt and pepper. Continue to cook until flavors have blended and vegetables are well done, about 15 minutes. If necessary, thin with water.

5. Serve in soup bowls and garnish each bowl with some grated egg. Serves 6 to 8.

I like this with lightly toasted whole wheat bread, followed by cheese and fresh fruit.

This hearty soup is a meal in itself. Most who first taste it cannot believe it is not made from a meat stock.

Savory Lentil Soup

1 pound lentils
1 onion, chopped
1 clove garlic, mashed
2 tablespoons olive oil
3 or 4 carrots, scraped and diced
1 15½-ounce can whole tomatoes and juice, coarsely chopped
½ teaspoon dried marjoram
¼ teaspoon summer savory
¼ teaspoon ground thyme
salt
¼ teaspoon white pepper
1 pound chopped fresh spinach (or 1 10-ounce package frozen)
¼ cup chopped parsley
1 cup grated Monterey Jack cheese

1. Cook lentils according to basic directions (see pages 23–26).

2. In a skillet, sauté onion and garlic in olive oil. Add carrots, tomatoes, herbs, and seasonings. Simmer until carrots are tender.

3. Combine the tomato mixture with the lentils and lentil broth. Add spinach. Bring soup to a boil, turn heat on low, and simmer for a few minutes to blend flavors and cook spinach.

4. Add parsley and cheese. Cook and stir until cheese melts. Serves 8.

I serve this with whole wheat bread and a tossed salad.

On a cold winter day, you cannot beat this warming repast.

Green Split Pea and Barley Vegetable Soup

¾ pound green split peas
½ cup barley
1 large onion, chopped
1 clove garlic, mashed
2 tablespoons butter
4 carrots, sliced
1 cup green beans, cut in ½-inch lengths
1 cup tomatoes, peeled and chopped
2 cups cauliflower flowerettes
¼ cup chopped parsley
salt
¼ teaspoon white pepper

1. Cook split peas according to basic directions (see pages 23–26). Drain most of the broth and reserve.

2. Cook barley in lightly salted water until tender. Drain, reserving cooking water.

3. Sauté onion and garlic in butter, in a kettle, until onion is transparent.

4. Add to the kettle, carrots, green beans, tomatoes, and split pea broth. Cook until the vegetables are almost tender.

5. Add cauliflower and parsley and continue cooking until cauliflower and all vegetables are tender.

6. Add split peas, cooked barley, salt, and pepper to the soup. Cook an additional 10 minutes. Add barley water if soup is too thick. Serves 6.

I like whole wheat potato rolls with this soup.

This hearty soup is filled with nutritious and flavorful ingredients.

Canadian Yellow Pea Soup

1 pound yellow split peas
2 tablespoons butter
2 leeks, washed well and sliced
2 stalks celery with some leaves, sliced
2 carrots, scraped and sliced
1 turnip, sliced
1 clove garlic, mashed
1 cup water
2 tablespoons thick tomato puree
2 bay leaves
3 cloves
⅛ teaspoon nutmeg
¼ teaspoon marjoram
¼ teaspoon tarragon
salt
⅛ teaspoon white pepper

1. Cook split peas according to basic directions (see pages 23–26). Simmer until they are very soft.

2. In a large saucepan, sauté in butter, leeks, celery, carrots, turnip, and garlic about 3 minutes. Add water, tomato puree, and seasonings. Cook until all vegetables are tender.

3. Combine vegetable mixture with split peas. Add more water, if necessary. Cook about 10 minutes. Adjust seasonings. Serves 8.

Hot corn bread goes well with this soup. A warm fruit compote is a pleasant ending to this satisfying meal.

This recipe for pasta e fagioli (macaroni and beans) is a thick, filling, and delicious soup.

Pasta e Fagioli Soup

½ pound dried great northern beans
3 tablespoons olive oil
1 onion, chopped
2 cloves garlic, mashed
1 cup coarsely chopped celery
1 carrot, grated
2 bay leaves
½ teaspoon oregano
¼ teaspoon crushed red pepper
1 large tomato, peeled and chopped (or ½ cup canned)
6 cups vegetable broth (may be made with vegetable bouillon cubes)
½ pound ditalini or other small pasta
salt
1 tablespoon chopped fresh basil (or 1 teaspoon dried)
¼ cup chopped parsley
grated Romano or Parmesan cheese

1. Cook beans according to basic directions (see pages 23–26). Drain, reserving broth.

2. Heat olive oil in a soup kettle over medium-high heat. Add onion, garlic, celery, carrot, bay leaves, oregano, and red pepper. Sauté and stir until onion is limp but not brown.

3. Add tomato, vegetable broth, and 1 cup of bean broth. Cook until vegetables are soft.

4. Cook ditalini according to directions on package. Drain and add to kettle with beans, salt, basil, and parsley.

5. Bring to a boil, reduce heat, and simmer 10 minutes. Add bean broth or water if soup is too thick. Serve immediately to 4 or 6. Pass cheese at the table.

An endive salad with an olive oil and wine vinegar dressing is a refreshing course to follow. Italian whole wheat bread is a welcome addition.

Be creative when preparing this traditional soup. Any variety of beans and any combination of vegetables may be used. Minestrone is always satisfying.

Minestrone

¼ pound red kidney beans
¼ pound great northern beans
1 large onion, chopped
1 leek, washed and diced
1 large clove garlic, mashed
3 tablespoons olive oil
1 cup peeled and chopped tomatoes
1 rounded tablespoon tomato paste
1 quart vegetable broth or bouillon
½ pound green beans, cut in ½-inch lengths
2 carrots, thinly sliced
1 zucchini, quartered lengthwise, then sliced
6 cups chopped celery and leaves
4 cups chopped cabbage
2 rounded tablespoons chopped parsley
1 rounded tablespoon chopped fresh basil (or 1 teaspoon dried)
¼ pound ditalini macaroni
salt
½ teaspoon white pepper
grated Romano or Parmesan cheese

1. Cook beans according to basic directions (see pages 23–26). Drain, reserving broth.

2. In a large kettle, sauté onion, leek, and garlic in olive oil until lightly browned.

3. Add tomatoes, tomato paste, bean broth, and vegetable broth. (Use stock you may have on hand or make some using vegetable bouillon cubes.) Bring to a boil.

4. Add green beans, carrots, zucchini, celery, cabbage, parsley, and basil. Simmer for 45 minutes.

5. Bring up the heat and add ditalini. Boil gently for 10 minutes, stirring occasionally.

6. Add kidney and great northern beans, salt, and pepper, and simmer 5 minutes longer. Add water to thin soup if necessary. Adjust seasonings. Add cheese at the table. Serves 6.

Eat with whole wheat Italian bread.

One of my favorite combinations—this soup is hearty and takes little time to prepare.

Italian Lentil and Escarole Soup

1 pound lentils
¼ cup olive oil
2 cloves garlic, halved lengthwise
1 onion, chopped
1 teaspoon oregano
1 head escarole or endive, washed and cut in 2-inch lengths
3 cups water
salt
¼ teaspoon cayenne
grated Romano cheese

1. Cook lentils according to basic directions (see pages 23–26), using 7 cups water.

2. In a soup kettle, heat olive oil and brown garlic pieces on both sides.

3. Add onion and oregano and sauté until onion is soft and lightly browned. Garlic pieces may be removed if desired.

4. Add escarole and water. Cook about 10 minutes or until escarole is tender.

5. Add lentils, with their cooking broth, salt, and cayenne. Let soup cook for 10 minutes to allow flavors to blend.

6. Pass cheese at the table. Serves 8.

I like a crusty, whole wheat Italian bread served with this. A salad of julienne cut beets with a little onion and a dressing of olive oil, wine vinegar, and oregano makes a colorful addition to the meal.

This French soup has a rich flavor, and the added attraction of an easy preparation. La voila!

Potage aux Haricots Blancs et Champignons

(White Bean and Mushroom Soup)

½ pound dried great northern beans
¾ pound (2 cups) sliced mushrooms
3 tablespoons butter
1 onion, chopped
1 clove garlic, mashed
½ cup diced carrots
¼ teaspoon thyme
¼ teaspoon marjoram
salt
⅛ teaspoon white pepper
3 cups vegetable broth (vegetable bouillon cubes may be used)
1 cup light cream or half and half

1. Cook beans according to basic directions (see pages 23–26). Do not drain.

2. In a soup kettle, lightly brown mushrooms in 2 tablespoons of the butter. Remove and reserve mushrooms.

3. In the remaining butter, sauté onion, garlic, and carrots. Do not allow to brown.

4. Add thyme, marjoram, salt, pepper, and vegetable broth, and simmer until vegetables are tender.

5. Set aside 1 cup of the beans. Put the remaining beans and bean broth into blender and blend until smooth.

6. A few minutes before serving, add the bean puree to the kettle, along with the reserved beans and mushrooms, and bring to boil. Boil 2 minutes and add cream. Do not allow to boil after cream has been added. When soup reaches the boiling point, serve immediately to 4.

Whole wheat toast or French bread goes well with this, as does a tossed salad with a French oil and vinegar dressing.

This elegant lentil soup from Alsace, France, can also be made with navy beans, in which case it is called Bohnesupp.

Linsesupp

½ pound lentils
1 leek, chopped
3 carrots, cut in small cubes
2 potatoes, diced
1 onion, uncut and stuck with 2 cloves
1 tablespoon chopped parsley
1 bay leaf
salt
⅛ teaspoon white pepper
water
2 vegetable bouillon cubes
1 cup half and half or light cream

1. Cook lentils according to basic directions (see pages 23–26) in a soup kettle.

2. In a large saucepan, put prepared vegetables, bay leaf, salt, pepper, and enough water to cover vegetables and bring to a boil. Reduce heat and simmer until vegetables are tender.

3. Add bouillon cubes and dissolve. Pour vegetables and broth into the kettle of lentils and lentil broth. Cook together for 5 minutes.

4. Add cream. Bring to the boiling point, but do not allow to boil. Serve immediately to 4 to 6.

Toasted whole wheat bread and a mild cheese are perfect accompaniments.

The tang of vinegar makes this a spirited soup.

Greek Lentil Soup

1 pound lentils
1 large onion, chopped
3 stalks celery, chopped
3 bay leaves
½ cup olive oil
2 cups canned Italian plum tomatoes, chopped, undrained
2 teaspoons oregano
2 tablespoons wine vinegar
salt
⅛ teaspoon white pepper

1. Cook lentils according to basic directions (see pages 23–26).

2. In a soup kettle, sauté onion, celery, and bay leaves in olive oil.

3. When onion is limp, add tomatoes and oregano. Cook until vegetables are well done.

4. Shortly before serving, add lentils and cooking broth, vinegar, salt, and pepper. Bring to a boil, reduce heat and cook 10 to 15 minutes. Serves 8.

I like to have whole wheat bread with this soup. I also like a Greek salad made with romaine lettuce, tomato wedges, cucumber slices, feta cheese, and Greek olives. Top the salad with a lemon juice and olive oil dressing and a pinch of oregano.

This spicy, orange-colored soup has an enticing cheddar flavor.

Creamy Mexican Soup

½ pound dried lima beans
2 tablespoons peanut oil
1 onion, chopped
1 clove garlic, mashed
1 small hot chili pepper, seeded and chopped
¼ teaspoon cayenne
1 tablespoon paprika
½ teaspoon ground cumin
¼ teaspoon oregano
1 cup thick tomato puree
2 tablespoons chopped fresh coriander (optional)
2 cups milk
2 cups grated sharp cheddar cheese
6 corn tortillas, cut in 1 x 3-inch strips

1. Cook beans according to basic directions (see pages 23–26).

2. Heat peanut oil in a large saucepan and sauté onion, garlic, pepper, and spices until onion is lightly browned. Stir occasionally.

3. Add tomato puree and coriander and simmer until onion is soft.

4. Combine beans and bean broth with tomato mixture and put in blender. Blend until smooth and return to saucepan.

5. Add milk and cheese. Cook, stirring occasionally, until soup reaches the boiling point. Serve immediately with fried corn tortilla strips. Serves 4.

6. While soup is cooking, fry corn tortilla strips in hot oil until lightly browned and crisp (see recipe for tortilla chips page 36). Serve with soup.

A lettuce, tomato, cucumber, and avocado salad with an oil and lemon juice dressing provides a pleasant contrast following the soup.

Sopa de Garbanzos

½ pound garbanzo beans (chick-peas)
6 6-inch corn tortillas
oil for frying tortillas
2 tablespoons peanut oil
1 large onion, chopped
2 cloves garlic, mashed
4 cups zucchini squash, quartered lengthwise, then thinly sliced
2 cups peeled and chopped tomatoes
1 cup concentrated, seasoned vegetable broth or 4 vegetable bouillon
   cubes, dissolved in 1 cup hot water
1 teaspoon oregano
¼ teaspoon cumin
¼ teaspoon liquid fructose sugar
1 or 2 jalapeño or other small hot peppers, seeded and chopped
salt
2 heaping tablespoons chopped fresh cilantro (coriander)
2 cups milk
1½ cups shredded Monterey Jack cheese

1. Cook garbanzo beans according to basic directions (see pages 23–26). Drain, reserving bean broth.

2. Cut tortillas in ½-inch wide strips, then cut strips in half. Fry strips in ⅛ inch hot frying oil for about 1 minute or until they are crisp and lightly browned. Drain on paper towels. Reserve.

3. In a soup kettle, heat peanut oil and sauté onion and garlic until onion is transparent. Add zucchini and continue to sauté vegetables until they are lightly browned.

4. Add tomatoes, broth, oregano, cumin, fructose, hot pepper, and reserved bean broth. Bring to a boil, lower heat, and simmer for 30 minutes or until soft.

5. Add the garbanzos, salt, cilantro, and milk and bring to the boiling point.

6. Add the cheese and stir until it melts.

7. Put a few tortilla strips in each soup bowl. Ladle soup over. Serves 4 to 6.

Additional warm, buttered tortillas may be served with the soup; guacamole goes well, too. Some of the crisped tortilla strips may be used to dip into the guacamole.

This delicious soup looks very attractive served in plain white or light-colored soup bowls.

Cuban Black Bean Soup

1 pound black beans
1 large onion, chopped
1 large (or 2 medium) cloves garlic, mashed
2 cups chopped celery with some leaves
2 jalapeño or other hot chili peppers, finely chopped
1 green pepper, chopped
3 tablespoons olive oil
6 whole cloves
½ teaspoon ground cumin
3 vegetable bouillon cubes
salt
2 tablespoons lemon juice
lemon slices
hard-boiled egg slices

1. Cook beans according to basic directions (see pages 23–26) until they are very soft.

2. In a skillet, sauté onion, garlic, celery, jalapeño and green pepper in olive oil with cloves and cumin until onion is golden.

3. Add some bean broth to the skillet and dissolve the bouillon cubes in the liquid.

4. Add salt and lemon juice. Simmer until vegetables are soft.

5. Mash some of the beans with a potato masher and pour contents from skillet into pan containing beans and bean broth.

6. Bring soup to a boil, lower heat, and simmer for 5 to 10 minutes to blend flavors. Add water if too thick. Adjust salt. When soup is piping hot, serve in warmed soup bowls and garnish with a lemon slice and a slice of hard-boiled egg. Serves 8.

With this soup, I like whole wheat raisin bread and a side dish of buttered spinach.

This is another enticing version of black bean soup.

Puerto Rican Black Bean Soup

1 pound black beans
¼ cup olive oil
2 onions, chopped
4 cloves garlic, mashed
3 green peppers, chopped
1 hot chili pepper, chopped
1 carrot, scraped and chopped
2 bay leaves
1 teaspoon oregano
½ teaspoon cumin
salt
⅛ teaspoon cayenne
2 tablespoons vinegar
1 cup cooked rice
½ cup green onions, chopped (reserve for garnish)

1. Cook beans according to basic directions (see pages 23–26), using 8 cups water, until beans are very soft.

2. In a large skillet, sauté in olive oil, until lightly browned, onions, garlic, green and chili peppers, and carrot.

3. Add bay leaves, oregano, cumin, salt, cayenne, and vinegar. Cook until vegetables are soft.

4. Shortly before serving, combine vegetables with the beans. Cook 10 minutes to blend flavors.

5. To serve, ladle soup into individual bowls. Place a large spoon of rice in the center of the bowl on top of soup and sprinkle with green onions. Serves 8.

A pleasant accompaniment with this soup are sliced avocados, sliced cheese, and whole wheat toast.

There are many good versions of lentil soup, but this one is exceptional.

Shorabat Addas

(Middle Eastern Lentil Soup)

1 pound lentils
¼ cup olive oil
1 large onion, chopped
½ teaspoon ground cumin
1 pound spinach, chopped (Swiss chard or beet greens are also
  delicious)
salt
¼ teaspoon white pepper
¼ cup lemon juice

1. Cook lentils according to basic directions (see pages 23–26), in 7 cups water until soft.

2. Heat olive oil in a soup kettle and fry onion until lightly browned. Add cumin, the cooked lentils and their broth, the spinach, and an additional cup of water. Bring to a boil, reduce heat, and simmer 10 minutes to allow spinach to cook and flavors to blend.

3. Add salt, pepper, and lemon juice. Cook an additional 5 minutes. Serves 6 to 8.

Serve warmed pita bread and a delicate flavored cheese with this soup.

The deep orange color, highlighted with bits of red and green, makes this soup attractive to look at and tempting to eat.

Ezo Gelin Soup

(Turkish Wedding Soup)

1 pound red lentils
8 tablespoons butter
2 large onions, chopped
4 cloves garlic, crushed
½ teaspoon cayenne
1 teaspoon paprika
1 teaspoon ground coriander
2 cups tomatoes, peeled and chopped
2 rounded tablespoons tomato paste
salt
1 tablespoon lemon juice
1 tablespoon chopped fresh mint (or 1 teaspoon dried)

1. Cook red lentils according to basic directions (see pages 23–26), using 8 cups water, until lentils are very soft and disintegrating.

2. In a soup kettle, melt 2 tablespoons of the butter over medium-low heat and sauté onions and garlic with cayenne, paprika, and coriander until onions are soft but not browned.

3. Add tomatoes and tomato paste and continue to cook for 20 minutes.

4. Shortly before serving, add lentils and cooking broth, salt, and lemon juice. Bring to a boil, reduce heat and cook 15 minutes.

5. Melt remaining 6 tablespoons butter with the mint. Dribble some mint butter over individual servings of soup. Serves 8.

I like to serve this soup with whole wheat bread and a mild cheese. A compote of stewed fruits is a pleasant ending to this delightful meal.

The combination of mint and dill gives this thick, nutritious soup a wonderfully different flavor.

Osh

(Afghanistan Beans and Noodles Soup)

1 cup mixed, dried beans (⅓ cup great northerns, ⅓ cup red kidneys, ⅓ cup chick-peas)
1 large onion, chopped
1 clove garlic, mashed
¼ cup olive oil
¼ teaspoon crushed red pepper
½ cup tomato puree
½ cup water
½ teaspoon dried mint
½ teaspoon dried dill
salt
¼ pound egg noodles
½ cup plain yoghurt
¼ cup water

1. Cook beans separately according to basic directions (see pages 23–26).

2. Fry onion and garlic in oil until lightly browned. Add crushed red pepper, and when it turns dark red, add tomato puree, water, dried mint, dried dill, and salt. Simmer while noodles cook.

3. Cook noodles in lightly salted boiling water until just tender. Drain.

4. Thin yoghurt with ¼ cup water.

5. Combine beans and bean broth with tomato sauce, noodles, and yoghurt. Adjust seasonings. When soup is piping hot, serve. Makes 4 servings.

This can be eaten with brown raisin bread and followed by a tossed salad with an oil and lemon juice dressing.

Another popular soup in Afghanistan is Mosh Awa, with its unusual combination of mung beans and chick-peas. It has an exotic flavor.

Mosh Awa

½ cup whole mung beans
½ cup chick-peas
1 large onion, chopped
1 clove garlic, mashed
¼ cup olive oil
¼ to ½ teaspoon crushed red pepper
½ cup tomato puree
¾ cup water
½ teaspoon dried mint
½ teaspoon dried dill
salt
½ cup plain yoghurt
¼ cup water

1. Cook mung beans and chick-peas separately, following the basic directions (see pages 23–26), until very soft. The mung beans will take less time to cook.

2. Fry onion and garlic in olive oil until lightly browned. Add crushed red pepper and cook another few seconds or until pepper turns a deep red. Add tomato puree, water, dried mint, dried dill, and salt. Cook until onion is very soft.

3. Add the beans and bean broth to the tomato sauce. Bring to a boil. Lower heat.

4. Thin yoghurt with the water and add to the soup. When it is piping hot, serve to 4.

We like this with homemade whole wheat raisin bread and a salad.

Chinese cuisine of the Szechwan style has become very popular in recent years. One of the great favorites is hot and sour soup, which features bean curd as its main ingredient. The ingredients can be purchased in stores where Oriental foods are sold.

Hot and Sour Soup

4 dried black mushrooms
6 dried wood ears
6 Tiger Lily buds
2 ounces bean thread noodles (also called cellophane noodles)
6 cups vegetable broth (vegetable bouillon cubes may be used)
1 carrot, coarsely grated
3 tablespoons tamari soy sauce
3 tablespoons Chinese rice vinegar
¼ to ½ teaspoon cayenne pepper
½ cup bamboo shoots, cut into matchsticks
2 tablespoons sliced scallions
½ pound doufu (bean curd), cut into matchsticks
1 tablespoon cornstarch, dissolved in ½ cup water
1 teaspoon liquid fructose sugar
1 teaspoon sesame seed oil
salt
1 lightly beaten egg

1. Rinse mushrooms, wood ears, and Tiger Lily buds and soak in 2 cups hot water for 30 minutes.

2. Soak bean thread noodles in warm water.

3. Bring vegetable broth to a boil and add carrot, tamari, vinegar, and cayenne. Simmer 5 minutes.

4. Add bamboo shoots, scallions, and bean curd.

5. Drain mushrooms, wood ears, and Tiger Lily buds, reserving soaking water. Cut stems from mushrooms and discard. Slice mushrooms and wood ears thinly and tie a knot in each Tiger Lily bud. Add all to soup.

6. Drain bean threads, cut in 4-inch lengths and add to soup.

7. Add dissolved cornstarch, fructose, sesame seed oil, and salt. Bring to a boil. If soup becomes too thick, add some of the reserved mushroom soaking liquid.

8. Just before serving, bring soup to a boil, add egg and stir gently with a fork. Serve immediately. Serves 6.

Many do not realize that in Japanese cuisine noodles are almost as important as rice. Noodle soup is a popular dish.

Japanese Noodle Soup with Tofu

7 cups hot water
2 strips of dried kombu seaweed about 3 × 8 inches
4 dried mushrooms
½ cup light soy sauce
½ cup vegetable bouillon
1 teaspoon liquid fructose sugar
salt
dash white pepper
1 leek, washed well and thinly sliced
1 carrot, scraped and thinly sliced
1 small (½ cup) bamboo shoot, thinly sliced
¼ cup fresh or frozen peas
½ pound tofu (bean curd), cut in ½-inch cubes
¼ pound spinach
½ cup chives, cut in ¼-inch lengths
about 7 ounces Japanese noodles—soba (made with buckwheat
    flour), udon (a flat noodle similar to linguine), or somen (a very thin
    noodle like vermicelli)
shichimi—a seasoning containing seven spices (optional)

1. Prepare dashi (soup base): Bring 6 cups of the water to a boil. Lightly wipe the kombu strips with a damp cloth, briefly pass them over a heated element to bring out the fragrance, and drop them into the water. Remove pan from heat and stir. Allow kombu to steep for 3 or 4 minutes, as with tea, to release its flavor. Remove kombu and return dashi to heat source.

2. Rinse and soak mushrooms in remaining 1 cup hot water for 30 minutes or until soft. Remove mushroom stems and discard. Slice mushrooms thinly and add to dashi with mushroom soaking liquid.

3. Add soy sauce, bouillon, fructose, salt, and pepper. Bring to a boil, reduce heat, and simmer 10 minutes.

4. Add leek, carrot, and bamboo shoot. Cook 5 minutes.

5. Add peas and tofu. Cook 2 minutes.

6. Add spinach leaves and chives and cook 1 more minute.

7. Cook the noodles: Bring to a boil plenty of water in a large saucepan. Do not add salt. When water boils hard, add noodles and stir. When the water reaches a boil again, add 1 cup of cold water. Bring to the boil again and test noodles. Cook until noodles are just tender, but not soft. Drain in a colander and briefly rinse under running water. If noodles become cold, reheat them by pouring boiling water over them in a colander.

8. Distribute some of the hot noodles among 4 or 5 soup bowls. Spoon vegetables and broth over noodles. Pass the shichimi at the table for additional flavor, if desired.

Toshie Mori from Tokyo, Japan, a piano student in Boston and frequent visitor to our home, has made for us this specialty from her country. We all enjoy the flavor and the healthful qualities of red miso soup. Kombu, miso, and compressed mochi can be purchased in stores where Oriental foods are sold.

Miso Soup with Spinach and Mochi

8 cups water
2 strips kombu seaweed about 3 × 8 inches
⅓ cup red miso
1 teaspoon liquid fructose sugar
6 rectangles, 1½ × 2½ inches, compressed mochi rice
8 ounces spinach leaves

1. Prepare dashi (soup base): Bring water to a boil. Lightly wipe the kombu strips with a damp cloth, briefly pass them over a heated element to bring out the fragrance, and drop them into the water. Remove from heat and stir for 3 or 4 minutes to release the flavor. Remove kombu.

2. Return dashi to the heat and add miso and fructose. Stir to dissolve miso.

3. Add compressed mochi. When mochi is soft, add spinach. Simmer 5 minutes and serve to 6. Spoon out one piece of mochi for each bowl and add spinach and soup.

I frequently have a cup of hot miso in the afternoon instead of coffee or tea. It is a satisfying and pleasant tasting drink.

Quick Miso Cup

1 tablespoon miso
1 cup boiling water
chives (optional)

1. Spoon miso into a mug or bowl and fill with boiling water. Stir to dissolve miso.

2. A few snipped chives on top is a tasty addition.

Salads

Salads

Everyone loves bean salads at picnics and potluck suppers. This is an all-time favorite.

Five Bean Salad

½ cup dried kidney beans (about 1½ cups cooked)
½ cup dried chick-peas
1 10-ounce package frozen lima beans
4 cups green beans, cut in 1-inch lengths
4 cups wax beans, cut in 1-inch lengths
½ large (or 1 medium) red onion, thinly sliced
½ cup sliced pimientos
1 large green pepper, thinly sliced
1 cup thinly sliced celery
Dressing:
   ⅓ cup liquid fructose sugar
   1 cup apple cider vinegar
   ⅓ cup vegetable oil
   salt
   dash white pepper

1. Cook dried beans separately, according to basic directions (see pages 23–26) until thoroughly cooked but still firm. Drain and chill.

2. Cook frozen lima beans according to directions on package. Drain and chill.

3. Steam green and wax beans until tender-crisp. Chill.

4. Combine all chilled beans with sliced onion, pimientos, green pepper, and celery.

5. Combine fructose, vinegar, oil, salt, and pepper. Pour over bean salad. Toss. Chill and toss again. Serves 12.

This is wonderful for a summer lunch or supper, and it is popular at picnics.

Rice and Bean Salad

2 cups cold, cooked beans (any kind), drained
4 cups cold, cooked brown rice
1 cup chopped celery
½ cup chopped cucumber
2 scallions, chopped
1 green pepper, chopped
1 tomato, diced
2 hard-boiled eggs, chopped
½ cup mayonnaise
1 teaspoon prepared mustard
salt
¼ teaspoon paprika
lettuce leaves

1. Combine all ingredients, except lettuce.
2. Mound the salad on a lettuce-lined platter. Sprinkle additional paprika over. Serves 4 to 6.

Muffins go nicely with this salad.

Everyone loves this! It has such a fresh taste.

Macaroni Salad

½ pound pink or red beans
1 pound ditalini macaroni
¼ cup sliced scallions
1 cup thinly sliced celery
1 cup salad olives, coarsely chopped
1 cup chopped fresh tomatoes
1 cup chopped green peppers
1 tablespoon chopped fresh basil
2 rounded tablespoons chopped fresh parsley
⅓ cup olive oil
¼ cup wine vinegar
salt
white pepper

1. Cook beans according to basic directions (see pages 23–26). Drain.

2. Cook macaroni in salted, boiling water. Drain in colander.

3. Place macaroni in large bowl. Add beans, other vegetables, and herbs.

4. Mix oil, vinegar, salt, and pepper. Pour over macaroni mixture and toss well. Serves 8 to 10.

This can be served chilled or at room temperature.

The fresh mint and subtle garlic flavors make this a delectable salad.

Green and White Bean Salad

¾ cup dried white beans (great northerns, white kidneys, or marrows)
5 cups fresh green beans, cut in 1-inch lengths, cooked
2 tablespoons chopped fresh mint leaves
2 cloves garlic, halved
salt
white pepper
⅓ cup olive oil
¼ cup wine vinegar

1. Cook white beans according to basic directions (see pages 23–26). They should not be too soft. Drain.

2. Place white beans in a bowl with 1 tablespoon of the mint, 2 pieces of the garlic, salt, and pepper.

3. In another bowl, put cooked green beans, 1 tablespoon of the mint, the other 2 pieces of garlic, salt, and pepper.

4. Combine olive oil and vinegar. Pour ½ over white beans and ½ over green beans. Stir. Refrigerate beans, stirring occasionally, until well chilled.

5. Just before serving, combine the two beans and toss gently. Adjust salt and remove garlic pieces if desired. Serves 6.

This hearty salad can be a meal itself when served with a substantial brown bread.

Mozzarella-Bean Salad

2 cups leftover baked beans or 1 can vegetarian beans in tomato sauce
2 green onions, chopped
1 small (or ½ medium) green pepper, chopped
1 small cucumber, halved lengthwise, then thinly sliced
1 small zucchini, halved lengthwise, then thinly sliced
2 tablespoons olive oil
1 tablespoon wine vinegar
¼ teaspoon oregano
1 cup diced mozzarella cheese
lettuce leaves

1. Combine all ingredients, except cheese and lettuce, in a bowl and chill.
2. Before serving, add cheese cubes and toss salad lightly.
3. Line a salad bowl or individual salad plates with lettuce leaves and heap salad on lettuce. Serves 4.

This salad has an appealing, fresh flavor.

Beans and Mushrooms Vinaigrette

⅔ cup dried red kidney beans (about 2 cups cooked)
3 cups green beans, cut in 1-inch pieces
1 cup sliced celery
1 cup thinly sliced mushrooms
1 tomato, cut in thin wedges
1 rounded tablespoon thinly sliced scallions
2 tablespoons chopped parsley
2 tablespoons chopped fresh basil
Dressing:
   1 teaspoon Dijon-style mustard
   2 tablespoons wine vinegar
   4 tablespoons olive oil
   salt
   dash white pepper
1 hard-boiled egg, cut in wedges, for garnish

1. Cook kidney beans according to basic directions (see pages 23–26). Drain and chill.

2. Steam green beans for 5 or 6 minutes, until tender-crisp. Chill.

3. Combine in a large bowl kidney beans, green beans, celery, mushrooms, tomato, scallions, parsley, and basil.

4. In a small jar, combine mustard, vinegar, olive oil, salt, and pepper. Shake well and pour over salad.

5. Toss salad and garnish with egg wedges. Serves 4 to 6.

When served with homemade muffins or popovers, this makes a delightful lunch.

Kidney Bean Salad

½ pound dried kidney beans
1 teaspoon finely minced green onion
½ cup thinly sliced celery
Dressing:
   2 tablespoons olive oil
   1 tablespoon wine vinegar
   1 small clove garlic, mashed
   salt
   white pepper
salad greens

1. Cook beans according to basic directions (see pages 23–26). Beans should not be too soft. Drain and chill.

2. Combine chilled beans with onion and celery. Mix dressing ingredients. Pour dressing over and mix gently but thoroughly.

3. Place salad greens on a plate and heap beans in center. Serves 4.

An attractive salad, this travels well to picnics and is always popular.

Kidney Bean Cabbage Salad

⅔ cup dried red kidney beans (about 2 cups cooked)
½ cup thinly sliced celery
1 rounded tablespoon thinly sliced green onion
1 cup thinly sliced green pepper, cut in ½-inch lengths
6 cups grated cabbage
Dressing:
   ¼ cup olive oil
   ¼ cup wine vinegar
   ¼ teaspoon liquid fructose sugar
   ¼ teaspoon dry mustard
   2 teaspoons salt
   ¼ teaspoon white pepper

1. Cook beans according to basic directions (see pages 23–26). Do not overcook. Drain and cool.

2. Place beans in large bowl with celery, green onion, green pepper, and cabbage.

3. Combine dressing ingredients and add to beans and other vegetables. Toss salad lightly. Chill. Serves 8 or more.

This attractive salad with its colorful ingredients should be made 12 to 24 hours ahead. When served in a deep, glass bowl, it will be the focal point at a luncheon.

Layered Salad

⅔ cup dried chick-peas
1 small head lettuce, coarsely shredded
1 cup thinly sliced fresh mushrooms
1 cup alfalfa sprouts
1 cup chopped green pepper
1 cup grated carrots
1 cup thinly sliced celery
½ cup thinly sliced scallions
1 10-ounce package frozen peas, thawed
4 hard-cooked eggs, sliced
salt
dash white pepper
1¼ cup mayonnaise
2 tablespoons milk
1½ cups grated cheddar cheese

1. Cook chick-peas according to basic directions (see pages 23–26). Drain.
2. Place lettuce on bottom of a large glass bowl. Over lettuce, layer evenly mushrooms, sprouts, green pepper, chick-peas, carrots, celery, scallions, peas, and eggs. Lightly salt and pepper the eggs.
3. Thin mayonnaise with milk and spread carefully over eggs.
4. Top with cheese. Do not mix.
5. Cover and refrigerate at least 12 and up to 24 hours. Serves 10 to 12.
I like to serve this satisfying salad with hot muffins.

The addition of chick-peas can enliven any vegetable salad. They are especially harmonious in this combination.

Spinach Salad with Chick-Peas and Mushrooms

½ cup dried chick-peas (about 1½ cups cooked)
5 tablespoons olive oil
2 tablespoons fresh lemon juice
salt
⅛ teaspoon white pepper
1 cup sliced raw mushrooms
¼ cup thinly sliced red onion
6 ounces fresh spinach, washed, well-drained, and broken into
   bite-sized pieces
1 hard-cooked egg, sliced

1. Cook chick-peas according to basic directions (see pages 23–26). Drain well and chill.

2. Combine oil, lemon juice, salt, and pepper in a large salad bowl. Add chick-peas, mushrooms, and onion slices and toss lightly. Add spinach and toss again.

3. Place egg slices attractively on top of salad. Serves 4 to 6.

Chick-pea salad, with a bowl of soup and some whole-grain bread, makes a delightful lunch.

Chick-Pea Salad

½ pound dried chick-peas
salt
1½ cups cherry tomatoes, halved
½ cup chopped green onions
1 tablespoon chopped fresh basil (optional)
Dressing:
   1 teaspoon lemon juice
   1 tablespoon wine vinegar
   1 tablespoon salad oil
   1 tablespoon olive oil
   dash hot pepper sauce
   dash paprika
   ⅛ teaspoon dried tarragon leaves
   salt
1 tablespoon chopped parsley

1. Cook chick-peas according to basic directions (see pages 23–26). Drain and lightly salt.

2. Place chick-peas in a shallow bowl. Distribute tomato halves, green onion, and basil over beans.

3. Prepare dressing and stir or shake well. Pour over salad and stir to distribute dressing evenly.

4. Sprinkle chopped parsley on top. Serves 4 to 6 as salad or first course.

This is a delightful salad to have in late summer when fresh tomatoes are at their best. I like to fill the tomatoes with salade Niçoise, tabbouleh, or rice and bean salad.

Fresh Tomato and Bean Salad

medium to large fresh tomatoes
lettuce leaves
bean salad
parsley or chives, chopped
olives for garnish

1. Core tomatoes and cut them from the top into eighths, but do not cut them all the way through.

2. Line salad plates with lettuce leaves and place a cut tomato on each plate. Spread out the wedges, keeping the bottom of the tomato intact.

3. Place a heap of bean salad on the center of each tomato and top with chopped parsley or chives. Add 2 or 3 olives to the salad plate for garnish.

Serve with muffins.

Legumes are a popular addition to the antipasto or "before the meal" course served with Italian dinners. Small white beans may be used in place of the lentils.

Italian Lentil Salad

1½ cups dried lentils
4 tablespoons olive oil
1 onion, chopped
1 clove garlic, mashed
3 tomatoes, peeled and chopped
1 teaspoon oregano
salt
⅛ teaspoon cayenne
3 tablespoons red wine vinegar
1 tablespoon chopped fresh basil
2 tablespoons chopped fresh Italian parsley

1. Cook lentils according to basic directions (see pages 23–26). After the lentils have soaked, bring to a boil and let boil for 1 minute. Test for doneness. If too hard, boil 1 more minute. They should not be overdone.

2. In a skillet, heat 2 tablespoons of the olive oil and sauté onion and garlic until golden.

3. Add tomatoes, oregano, salt, and cayenne. Cook until vegetables are thoroughly cooked.

4. Drain lentils and put into a bowl. Add the tomato mixture, vinegar, the remaining 2 tablespoons olive oil, basil, and parsley. Mix thoroughly but gently. Adjust salt and cool. Serves 6 to 8.

This salad is best served at room temperature. It can be part of an antipasto tray or mounded on romaine lettuce leaves. Serve as a salad or as a first course, with lightly toasted, whole wheat Italian bread.

Anne Muller, assistant conductor of the Toulouse Symphony and a wonderful cook, prepared this salad, a family favorite in her home in Strasbourg.

Salade Niçoise

1 cup dried navy or pea beans
2 tablespoons finely chopped onion
½ cup sliced green olives stuffed with pimientos
2 tablespoons capers
salt
dash white pepper
2 tablespoons olive oil
1 tablespoon wine vinegar
¼ teaspoon oregano
1 teaspoon chopped fresh basil (or ¼ teaspoon dried)

1. Cook beans according to basic directions (see pages 23–26), but not too soft. Rinse in cold water and drain.

2. Place beans in a bowl and add all other ingredients. Stir lightly but thoroughly. Place in refrigerator and serve when cold. Serves 6.

This makes an excellent first course. Serve with thinly sliced whole wheat bread, and perhaps a mild French cheese.

The colorful vegetables give this salad eye appeal as well as taste appeal.

Gazpacho Salad

½ pound dried baby lima beans
½ cup chopped green onions
1 cup diced green peppers
1 cucumber, diced
2 tomatoes, diced
1 avocado, diced
Dressing:
    ¼ cup olive oil
    ¼ cup wine vinegar
    1 small clove garlic, mashed
    ⅛ teaspoon ground cumin
    ¼ teaspoon oregano
    salt
    ⅛ teaspoon white pepper

1. Cook lima beans according to basic directions (see pages 23–26). Cook until tender but firm. Drain beans well and chill.

2. Combine beans with vegetables.

3. Combine dressing ingredients and pour over salad. Mix thoroughly but gently. Chill and serve to 6 or more.

Croutons sprinkled over the salad make a pleasing addition.

This is one of our favorite summertime meals and is easy to prepare.

Taco Salad

1 small head lettuce, thinly sliced
tortilla chips
½ recipe chili, warmed (see recipe, page 152)
6 ounces sharp cheddar cheese
4 fresh tomatoes, cut in wedges
2 avocados, sliced
green onions or chives, chopped
lemon juice
hot pepper sauce

1. Line 6 plates with lettuce.

2. Put some tortilla chips on the lettuce in the center of the plate.

3. Pour a couple of large spoonfuls of chili over the chips.

4. Sprinkle with grated cheddar.

5. Place tomato wedges and avocado slices decoratively on top of salad.

6. Sprinkle with green onions or chives and with a few drops of fresh lemon juice. Pass hot pepper sauce and additional tortilla chips at the table. Serves 6.

This tasty, healthful salad is a family favorite that I make frequently in summer.

Guacamole Salad

¾ cup dried red kidney beans
2 tablespoons salad oil
1 tablespoon lemon juice
salt
few drops hot pepper sauce
1 small head lettuce, coarsely shredded
1 large green pepper, chopped
3 tomatoes, chopped
1 scallion, thinly sliced
Dressing:
   1 large, ripe avocado, mashed
   ⅓ cup plain yoghurt
   2 tablespoons finely minced scallions
   ½ teaspoon salt
   1 teaspoon lemon juice
1 cup grated cheddar cheese
1 cup broken corn chips

1. Cook beans according to basic directions (see pages 23–26). Drain and add salad oil, lemon juice, salt, and hot pepper sauce. Stir well and refrigerate at least 1 hour. Drain again before using.

2. Combine lettuce, green pepper, tomatoes, and scallion in a large salad bowl. Chill.

3. Combine dressing ingredients and mix well.

4. Just before serving, put beans in salad. Spoon dressing over and sprinkle with cheese and corn chips. Toss the salad well. Serves 10 to 12.

Tabbouleh, a tasty and healthful salad and a specialty of Lebanon, has become popular far beyond the Middle East.

Tabbouleh

½ cup dried navy or pea beans
½ cup cracked wheat (medium)
3 cups chopped fresh parsley
½ cup chopped fresh mint
¼ cup finely chopped scallions
2 large (or 3 medium) tomatoes, cut in small cubes
⅛ teaspoon white pepper
⅛ teaspoon allspice
⅛ teaspoon cinnamon
salt
dash cayenne
½ cup olive oil
⅓ cup fresh lemon juice
romaine lettuce leaves

1. Cook beans according to basic directions (see pages 23–26). Drain in colander and rinse under cold water. Chill drained beans in refrigerator.

2. Soak cracked wheat in cold water for 30 minutes. Drain and chill.

3. Place all ingredients in a large bowl and mix gently but thoroughly. Chill. Serve heaped on romaine lettuce leaves. Serves 4.

Ethiopians are very religious, whether Christian or Muslim, and fasting is an important part of their lives. The Ethiopian church sprang from the third great center of Christianity in Alexandria, Egypt. Its members are obligated to fast many days of the year, and one of the strictest fasts is during the Lenten season before Easter. During this time, Ethiopian Christians are restricted from eating meat of any kind, animal fat, eggs, and milk. Hence, dried legumes have an especially important role in their diet.

Ethiopian Lentil Salad

½ pound dried lentils
¼ cup chopped shallots
1 3-ounce can chopped green chilies
2 fresh chilies, seeded and sliced in thin 1-inch long strips
1 tablespoon chopped fresh basil (or 1 teaspoon dried)
salt
3 tablespoons wine vinegar
3 tablespoons salad oil
tomato wedges (optional)

1. Cook lentils according to basic directions (see pages 23–26). After lentils have soaked, they will take only 1 or 2 minutes to cook. Do not overcook.

2. Briefly rinse lentils under cold water, drain, and place in a bowl. Add all remaining ingredients, except tomato, and mix thoroughly but gently.

3. Place in refrigerator and stir occasionally while salad is chilling. Garnish with tomato wedges if desired. Serves 4 to 6.

Pass whole wheat crackers, bread sticks, or rye krisp with salad.

This is a moist and flavorful salad.

Sweet and Sour Lentil Salad

½ pound lentils
1 onion, finely chopped
½ cup thinly sliced celery
½ cup peeled and chopped cucumber
½ cup chopped green pepper
1 tablespoon liquid fructose sugar
salt
⅛ teaspoon white pepper
2 teaspoons tamari soy sauce
¼ cup apple cider vinegar

1. Cook lentils according to basic directions (see pages 23–26). Cook only 1 or 2 minutes or until tender but firm. Drain all but ¼ cup lentil broth.

2. Combine lentils with remaining ingredients. Chill. Serves 4 to 6.

We enjoy this salad with avocado on toasted whole wheat English muffins.

This unusual salad combines lots of flavor and refreshing crunchiness with a high nutrition content.

Chinese Soybean Salad

1 cup dried soybeans
Marinade:
   2 tablespoons peanut oil
   1 tablespoon sesame seed oil
   1 tablespoon rice wine vinegar
   1 teaspoon Hoisin sauce
   2 tablespoons soy sauce
   1 clove garlic, mashed
   1 tablespoon grated ginger
   salt
   dash white pepper
4 cups sliced Chinese cabbage
1 cup bean sprouts
½ cup water chestnuts, cut in matchsticks
½ cup carrots, cut in matchsticks
2 tablespoons chopped chives or green onions

1. Cook soybeans according to basic directions (see pages 23–26). Drain well and put into a bowl.

2. Combine marinade ingredients in a jar and shake well. Pour over soybeans and mix thoroughly. Refrigerate beans for at least 1 hour.

3. Add remaining ingredients to soybeans, toss well and serve. Serves 6 or more.

Serve with whole wheat crackers, bread, or rice.

Main Dishes

United States of America

Ledy Washingdon

eXfelene georg general Washingdon

United States
of America

This traditional early American dish originated in Boston, but its popularity spread throughout the land. This meatless version is delicious.

Boston Baked Beans

1 pound navy or pea beans
2 onions, chopped
¼ pound butter
2 vegetable bouillon cubes
3 tablespoons granulated fructose sugar
¼ cup blackstrap molasses
1 teaspoon dry mustard
½ teaspoon white pepper
salt

1. Cook beans according to basic directions (see pages 23–26). Drain and reserve broth.

2. In a large saucepan, sauté onions in butter over medium heat until onions are soft and golden, about 10 minutes.

3. Dissolve bouillon cubes in 1 cup of the hot bean broth and add to saucepan with all remaining ingredients, including drained beans.

4. Mix well, bring to a boil, and pour into a 1½- or 2-quart bean pot or ceramic ovenproof dish.

5. Bake, uncovered, in a 325°F. oven about 1½ hours. Stir every 20 minutes and add more bean broth if mixture becomes too dry. Beans should remain moist. Serves 6.

I like to serve Boston brown bread with raisins and cole slaw with the beans. There is nothing traditional about this, but I usually have on the table a good French mustard, such as Pommery.

If you are wondering what to do with all that squash in your garden, try this.

Summer Squash Bake

1 cup dried navy or pea beans
1 large onion, chopped
1 hot chili pepper, finely chopped
1 tablespoon butter
2 yellow squash, sliced
2 white squash (sometimes called patty pan), sliced
2 medium-small zucchini squash, sliced
2 tablespoons peanut oil
2 cups bean sprouts
3 eggs, beaten
2 cups milk
salt
white pepper
1½ cups grated cheddar cheese

1. Cook beans according to basic directions (see pages 23–26). Drain.

2. Sauté onion and pepper in butter until lightly browned. Combine with drained beans and remove from heat.

3. In a large skillet, fry and stir squash in peanut oil until tender-crisp. Add sprouts and fry another minute. Reserve.

4. Combine eggs with milk.

5. Add salt and pepper to beans, to squash, and to eggs.

6. In a large, shallow, buttered casserole, spread bean mixture evenly on bottom. Then layer squash evenly over beans. Pour egg mixture over all.

7. Bake in 350°F. oven for approximately 45 minutes.

8. Sprinkle cheese over top and return to oven until cheese is melted, about 5 minutes. Serves 4.

Serve with corn bread and a tossed salad.

This simple casserole has a very pleasant flavor and is one you will want to make frequently.

Brown Rice, Bean, and Spinach Bake

1 cup dried great northern beans
¼ cup butter
1 medium onion, chopped
1 cup brown rice
2½ cups vegetable broth
1½ pounds fresh spinach (or 2 10-ounce packages frozen)
½ pound grated cheddar cheese
4 eggs, beaten
1 cup milk
½ teaspoon marjoram
½ teaspoon thyme
salt
⅛ teaspoon white pepper

1. Cook beans according to basic directions (see pages 23–26). Drain.

2. Heat ¼ cup butter in saucepan. Fry onion in butter until soft but not brown. Add rice and fry until rice is opaque. Add vegetable broth, bring to a boil, cover saucepan tightly, reduce heat, and barely simmer about 40 minutes or until rice is done.

3. Cook spinach, drain, and combine with rice mixture and all but ¾ cup of the cheese. Set aside the ¾ cup cheese for topping.

4. Combine eggs, milk, marjoram, thyme, salt, and pepper. Pour egg mixture and drained beans over rice.

5. Mix carefully, and pour into a buttered 2½-quart casserole dish. Bake at 350°F. for 45 minutes. Sprinkle remaining cheese on top and bake an additional 5 minutes. Serves 4.

This needs only a salad to follow it and perhaps a good brown bread or corn bread as an accompaniment.

A simple preparation with an elegant flavor, this puree is a good side dish to accompany a main course. For lunch, it can be served with salad and whole-grain bread.

Lima Bean Puree

½ pound dried lima beans
4 tablespoons butter
½ cup milk
salt
⅛ teaspoon white pepper

1. Cook lima beans according to basic directions (see pages 23–26) until very soft.
2. Drain limas and put beans into blender with butter, milk, salt, and pepper. Blend until smooth.
3. Pour back into pan and heat until puree is very hot. Serves 4.

Terri and David Sopher brought an attractive dish of succotash to our Thanksgiving dinner last year in Syracuse, New York. At first taste, we all agreed that Terri's recipe should have a place in this book. It was the best we have sampled of this famous American Indian dish.

Terri's Succotash

1 cup dried lima beans
⅔ cup chopped celery
1 onion, chopped
1 clove garlic, mashed
2 tablespoons butter
2 tablespoons flour
1 cup hot vegetable broth (vegetable bouillon cubes may be used)
2⅔ cups fresh or frozen corn kernels
salt
⅛ teaspoon white pepper
⅛ teaspoon nutmeg
½ cup cream
bread crumbs
butter

1. Cook beans according to basic directions (see pages 23–26). Drain.

2. Cook celery in a very small amount of water until tender.

3. Sauté onion and garlic in butter until onion is soft and golden but not browned.

4. Add flour to onions and cook while stirring until it is well blended. Add hot vegetable broth, all at once, and continue to cook and stir vigorously (a whisk works well) until sauce comes to a boil and is smooth.

5. Add beans, celery, corn, salt, pepper, and nutmeg. When mixture comes to the boil once again, add cream and adjust salt.

6. Pour into a buttered casserole dish. Sprinkle with bread crumbs and dot with butter.

7. Bake in 350°F. oven approximately 25 minutes or until bubbling and top is golden. Serves 4.

I like whole wheat raisin bread and a tossed salad with this.

This is an attractive and delicious casserole for company or family fare.

California Cheese and Chilies Casserole

½ pound dried baby lima beans
salt
dash cayenne
½ pound sharp cheddar cheese, grated
½ pound Monterey Jack cheese, grated
2 small cans chopped green chilies
½ cup sliced green onions
2 cups fresh or frozen corn kernels
4 eggs
2 tablespoons whole wheat flour
1¾ cups milk
1 or 2 fresh tomatoes, sliced

1. Cook beans according to basic directions (see pages 23–26). Drain.

2. Combine drained beans, salt, and cayenne in a deep, buttered, 3-quart casserole dish.

3. Reserve 1 cup grated cheddar cheese for the topping and stir into beans remaining cheddar, Monterey Jack cheese, chilies, green onions, and corn.

4. In a bowl, beat eggs and flour with a whisk or fork. Add milk, salt, and cayenne. Stir into bean mixture.

5. Top with tomato slices, cover, and bake in a 350°F. oven about 45 minutes or until inserted knife emerges clean.

6. Sprinkle reserved cheese over casserole and return to oven uncovered for 3 or 4 minutes to melt cheese. Serves 4 to 6.

Corn muffins and a tossed salad provide pleasing additions to the meal.

This easy-to-prepare dish is family or company fare.

Cheesey Limas and Broccoli

½ pound dried baby lima beans
salt
white pepper
1 bunch broccoli, cut into small pieces
2 tablespoons butter
3 tablespoons whole wheat flour
2 cups hot milk
1½ cups grated cheddar cheese
1 cup bread crumbs
2 tablespoons butter

1. Cook beans according to basic directions (see pages 23–26).

2. Drain beans and place them in a 2-quart casserole dish. Sprinkle with salt and pepper.

3. Steam broccoli 15 minutes and place evenly over beans.

4. In a saucepan, melt butter over low heat. Blend in

flour and cook for 2 minutes, stirring constantly. Add the milk and bring to a boil while stirring. When smooth, add salt to taste and cheese.

5. When cheese has melted, pour the sauce over the beans and broccoli.

6. Sprinkle bread crumbs over and dot with butter.

7. Place in 350°F. oven and bake until top is lightly browned and casserole is bubbling—about 30 minutes. Serves 4.

Serve with corn bread and a fruit salad.

Here is a delightful bean and cabbage combination in a sauce Parisienne.

Creamy Lima and Cabbage Casserole

1 pound dried baby lima beans
4 tablespoons butter
1 tablespoon peanut oil
½ onion, chopped
1 cup sliced celery
1 medium head (10 cups) cabbage, coarsely chopped
2 rounded tablespoons flour
2 cups hot milk
scant ¼ teaspoon nutmeg
salt
1 egg yolk
⅛ teaspoon white pepper
¼ cup grated Parmesan cheese

1. Cook lima beans according to basic directions (see pages 23–26). Drain.

2. Heat 2 tablespoons of the butter and the oil in a large saucepan. Add onion and cook until onion is transparent. Add celery and sauté until celery is tender but not brown. Gradually add cabbage, stirring until cabbage is wilted. Cover and cook over low heat about 10 minutes or until cabbage is tender.

3. In a second saucepan, heat remaining 2 tablespoons

of the butter until frothy. Add flour and cook and stir until well blended. Add milk, all at once, stirring constantly, and cook until sauce is thick and smooth. Add nutmeg and salt.

4. Beat egg yolk in a small bowl. Add a tablespoon of the sauce to the yolk and beat. Pour egg yolk mixture into the sauce and stir. Remove from heat.

5. In a large, shallow, buttered casserole dish, combine drained beans, vegetables, ½ the sauce, salt, and pepper.

6. Pour remaining sauce over casserole contents. Sprinkle with Parmesan cheese.

7. Bake in preheated 350°F. oven for 20 to 25 minutes or until bubbling.

8. Place under broiler for a minute or two until lightly browned. Serves 6 to 8.

Boiled potatoes and a tossed salad go well with this.

This takes some time to prepare; the results are well worth it.

Stuffed Cabbage

½ pound dried baby lima beans
1¼ cup brown rice
Tomato sauce:
  1 large onion, chopped
  1 large green pepper, chopped
  2 tablespoons olive oil
  5 cups peeled and chopped tomatoes
  ¼ teaspoon allspice
  salt
  ⅛ teaspoon cayenne
  1 tablespoon lemon juice
  ¼ cup chopped parsley
2 medium-large heads cabbage
½ cup pine nuts, lightly browned in a little butter (optional)
½ cup raisins (optional)
salt
⅛ teaspoon cayenne

1. Cook beans according to basic directions (see pages 23–26). Drain.

2. While beans are cooking, cook rice over low heat in double its volume of lightly salted water for 25 to 45 min-

utes or until water has evaporated and rice is tender.

3. To make tomato sauce, first sauté onion and pepper in olive oil until soft. Add tomatoes, seasonings, and lemon juice. Simmer 10 minutes. Add parsley and remove from heat.

4. Core the cabbage heads and drop into boiling water. Remove the leaves from the heads as they soften. You will need about 18 leaves.

5. Combine beans, rice, pine nuts, raisins, salt, cayenne, and enough tomato sauce to moisten mixture.

6. Into a 6-quart pan, pour about ¾ cup of tomato sauce evenly on the bottom.

7. Place about 2 rounded tablespoons of bean mixture on a cabbage leaf. Fold the bottom portion of the leaf over the filling, tuck in both sides of leaf and roll it up. Continue to fill and roll all cabbage leaves.

8. Place each roll in a pan, side by side, in one layer. Spoon some tomato sauce over rolls. Continue making layers of cabbage rolls and tomato sauce until all rolls are placed in pan.

9. Simmer 1 hour and serve steaming hot with remaining tomato sauce. Serves 6 to 8.

Serve with boiled potatoes and a fruit salad.

This easy-to-prepare dish has a genuine New Orleans flavor.

Creole Lima Beans

½ pound dried lima beans
1 tablespoons butter
1 medium onion, chopped
1 cup chopped green pepper
1 hot chili pepper, finely chopped
1 stalk celery, chopped
1 14-ounce can whole tomatoes, chopped
2 tablespoons tomato paste
salt
½ teaspoon granulated fructose sugar
¼ teaspoon thyme

1. Cook lima beans according to basic directions (see pages 23–26). Drain, reserving broth.

2. Heat butter in a large saucepan. Sauté onion, green pepper, and chili pepper until onion is golden.

3. Add celery, tomatoes, tomato paste, salt, fructose, and thyme. Cook about 15 minutes or until all vegetables are tender.

4. Add drained beans and simmer a few minutes longer. If too dry, add some reserved bean broth. When piping hot, serve to 4.

I like this over brown rice. A congealed salad is a pleasant addition.

In North Carolina, the "Tar Heel" state, this dish, with its piquant flavor, is very popular at church suppers. It is, however, enjoyed anytime.

Tar Heel Barbequed Baked Beans

1 pound dried pinto beans
3 onions—2 chopped, 1 thinly sliced
2 large green peppers, coarsely chopped
2 cloves garlic, mashed
2 tablespoons peanut oil
3 tablespoons prepared mustard
2 tablespoons chili powder
salt
1 8-ounce can tomato sauce
¼ cup chili sauce
½ cup cider vinegar
¼ cup raw sugar
dash hot pepper sauce

1. Cook beans according to basic directions (see pages 23–26). Drain, reserving 2 cups of the broth.

2. Cook chopped onions, green peppers, and garlic in peanut oil until onions are lightly browned. Add remaining ingredients, except sliced onion, and including beans and broth.

3. Pour into large, oiled casserole. Place the slices of onion evenly over the top and bake 45 to 60 minutes in 350°F. oven. Serves 6 to 8.

A good brown bread and cole slaw accompany this dish very well.

This dish from Houston, Texas, tastes great! It looks attractive, and kid's love it. You will want to make it often.

Urban Cowboy Special

½ pound dried pinto beans
1½ cups carrots sliced in ¼-inch discs
2 tablespoons peanut oil
2 onions, chopped
2 green peppers, diced
2 teaspoons chili powder (hot, Mexican-style)
½ teaspoon oregano
¼ teaspoon ground cumin
1 28-ounce can Italian plum tomatoes, chopped
½ cup water
salt
1 tablespoon chopped fresh coriander leaves
½ pound elbow macaroni
1½ cups grated cheddar cheese

1. Cook beans according to basic directions (see pages 23–26). Drain and keep warm.

2. Cook carrots in ¼ cup water until tender.

3. Heat peanut oil and fry onions and green pepper until onion is soft. Add chili powder, oregano, and cumin and sauté 3 minutes longer. Add tomatoes and water and cook until vegetables are tender. Add cooked carrots, drained beans, salt, and coriander. Simmer while cooking macaroni.

4. Cook macaroni in boiling, lightly salted water until tender but not too soft. Drain and combine with bean and tomato mixture.

5. Turn into an oiled casserole dish. Sprinkle cheese on top and put in a preheated 400°F. oven for a few minutes to melt the cheese. Serve immediately to 4 or more.

Corn bread and a tossed salad go well with this.

I especially like to prepare this dish in late summer when I am harvesting vegetables from our garden. Colache has a wonderful fresh flavor. I add whatever herbs I have in abundance.

Colache

½ pound pinto beans
2 cloves garlic, mashed
1 large onion, chopped
2 tablespoons olive oil
1 large green pepper, cut in large cubes
1 small hot chili pepper, chopped
3 cups sliced zucchini squash
3 cups sliced yellow squash
4 cups green beans, broken in 1-inch lengths
2 cups tomatoes, peeled and chopped
1 tablespoon vinegar
salt
2 cups fresh corn kernels, cut off cob (or 1 10-ounce package frozen)
½ cup fresh herbs, chopped

1. Cook beans according to basic directions (see pages 23–26). Drain and reserve ½ cup broth.

2. Sauté garlic and onion in olive oil until onion is transparent. Add green pepper and chili pepper and sauté 5 minutes longer. Add squash and sauté another 5 minutes.

3. Add green beans, tomatoes, vinegar, and salt. Simmer until vegetables are tender.

4. Add corn and pinto beans with ½ cup reserved bean broth. Bring to a boil, reduce heat, add herbs and cook 5 to 10 minutes to allow flavors to blend. Serve with steamed bulgur or rice. Serves 4 to 6.

Fresh fruit and cheese completes this meal very satisfactorily.

These easy-to-prepare beans are designed especially for break-fast, but are excellent for lunch, brunch, or supper. They are best served on buttered toast.

Beans on Toast

1 pound red kidney beans (or ½ pound red and ½ pound white
   kidney beans)
2 green onions, chopped
1 tablespoon butter
1 tablespoon lemon juice
2 tablespoons chopped parsley
salt

1. Cook beans according to basic directions (see pages 23–26). Cook separately if using both red and white beans. They should be cooked the evening before if you wish to serve them for breakfast, but no ingredients should be added to beans until shortly before serving them.

2. In a small saucepan, sauté green onions in butter until soft. Add lemon juice.

3. When beans are done, add the green onion mixture to them along with parsley and salt. Mix well. Serves 8.

Spoon beans over buttered whole wheat toast.

This practical recipe makes enough for two bean loaves. I serve one loaf hot from the oven with Spanish tomato sauce. The other I chill and serve cold the next day with curry mayonnaise. Recipes for Spanish tomato sauce and curry mayonnaise follow.

Red Bean Loaf

1 pound dried red beans
1 cup cooked bulgur or brown rice
1 cup grated carrots
1 cup finely chopped celery
1 large onion, chopped
4 eggs, slightly beaten
salt
⅛ teaspoon white pepper

100

1. Cook beans according to basic directions (see pages 23–26).

2. Drain and mash beans. Do not worry about lumps.

3. In a large bowl combine mashed beans with remaining ingredients and mix thoroughly.

4. Place mixture in two 9 × 5-inch oiled loaf pans and bake in preheated 350°F. oven for 60 to 70 minutes. Each loaf is enough for 4 to 6.

I serve whole wheat toast and a salad with the hot bean loaf and Spanish tomato sauce.

The cold bean loaf and curry mayonnaise is especially nice for lunch and goes well with popovers or muffins and a fresh fruit salad.

Although intended for serving with red bean loaf, this sauce can accompany several bean dishes requiring sauce.

Spanish Tomato Sauce

1 onion, chopped
½ green pepper, chopped
2 tablespoons olive oil
2 cups peeled and chopped tomatoes
dash cayenne
salt

1. Sauté onion and green pepper in olive oil until onion is transparent. Add remaining ingredients.

2. Simmer about 15 minutes or until vegetables are soft.

Serve with chilled red bean loaf, or with any cold cooked beans requiring a salad dressing.

Curry Mayonnaise

1 cup mayonnaise
½ teaspoon curry powder
½ teaspoon milk

Combine ingredients and chill.

This southern dish traditionally is made with the addition of pickled pork meat. The following meatless version is great!

Louisiana Red Beans and Rice

1 pound dried red kidney beans
3 tablespoons peanut oil
2 large onions, chopped
3 cloves garlic, mashed
2 large green peppers, chopped
3 large stalks celery, sliced
2 bay leaves
½ teaspoon thyme
¼ teaspoon cumin
1 teaspoon paprika
½ cup peeled and chopped tomatoes
1 tablespoon vinegar
hot pepper sauce to taste
salt

1. Cook beans according to basic directions (see pages 23–26).

2. Heat peanut oil in a large saucepan and sauté onions, garlic, green peppers, and celery. Add the bay leaves, thyme, cumin, paprika, tomatoes, vinegar, and some bean broth. Simmer vegetables until they are tender.

3. Shortly before serving, add the beans with the remaining broth, hot pepper sauce, and salt. Bring to a boil, lower heat, and simmer about 5 minutes. Serve over steaming rice. Serves 6 to 8.

Delicious with a green salad.

This attractive dish, with its contrasts of black, white, and bits of green, has a spicy, piquant flavor.

Southern Black Beans and Rice

1 pound dried black beans
¾ cup olive oil
1 onion, chopped
1 clove garlic, mashed
1 green pepper, coarsely chopped
2 bay leaves
1 teaspoon oregano
¼ teaspoon cumin
2 tablespoons plus ¼ cup wine vinegar
½ to 1 teaspoon hot pepper sauce
1 teaspoon honey
salt
hot cooked rice
chopped green onions

1. Cook beans according to basic directions (see pages 23–26). Drain, reserving ½ cup bean broth.

2. Heat ¼ cup of the olive oil and sauté onion, garlic, green pepper, and bay leaves until onion is lightly browned.

3. Add oregano, cumin, 2 tablespoons of the vinegar, and reserved bean broth. Simmer until onion and pepper are soft.

4. Shortly before serving, add drained beans, hot pepper sauce, honey, and salt. Bring to a boil, reduce heat, and simmer 10 minutes to allow flavors to blend.

5. Serve over rice topped with some green onions.

6. Combine ½ cup olive oil with ¼ cup wine vinegar and a pinch of salt in a covered jar. Shake well and spoon a little over each serving. Serves 6 to 8.

I like to serve lightly cooked carrots and a fruit salad with this.

This dish appears on my dinner table frequently because of its ease of preparation and the many compliments it brings.

Black-Eyed Pea Potpourri

1 pound dried black-eyed peas
2 cloves garlic, mashed
2 carrots, sliced
8 stalks celery with leaves, sliced
1 tablespoon olive oil
1 28-ounce can tomatoes, chopped
1 8-ounce can tomato sauce
2 bay leaves
salt
dash white pepper
1½ cups grated cheddar cheese

1. Cook black-eyed peas according to basic directions (see pages 23–26). Drain, reserving broth.

2. Sauté garlic, carrots, and celery in olive oil for 5 minutes. Add tomatoes, tomato sauce, bay leaves, and black-eyed pea broth. Cook until vegetables are tender but not too soft.

3. Add black-eyed peas, salt, and pepper, and cook 10 minutes longer.

4. Add cheddar cheese and serve when cheese has melted. Serves 6 to 8.

This is nice spooned over hot brown rice or bulgur and served with a salad.

This delicious and attractive combination of beans is one you will want to prepare often.

Mixed Beans with Tofu Mayonnaise

⅓ cup dried chick-peas
⅓ cup dried baby lima beans (or 1 cup fresh or frozen)
⅓ cup dried kidney beans
2 cups green beans, cut in 1-inch lengths
1 cup fresh or frozen peas
2 tablespoons butter
2 scallions, chopped
1 teaspoon lemon juice
salt
⅛ teaspoon white pepper

1. Cook dried beans separately, according to basic directions (see pages 23–26). Drain and combine in a large bowl.

2. Cook green beans until tender-crisp, drain, and add to the bowl.

3. Cook peas until just done, drain, and add to beans.

4. Heat butter in a small saucepan and sauté scallions until cooked but not brown. Add lemon juice.

5. Shortly before serving, pour the butter sauce over the mixed beans. Add salt and pepper and mix gently but thoroughly.

6. Beans should be served with tofu mayonnaise either at room temperature or cold, as a salad.

This high-protein, eggless mayonnaise is simple to prepare and has few calories. Eat heartily!

Tofu Mayonnaise

½ pound tofu (bean curd)
2 teaspoons Dijon-style mustard
½ teaspoon salt
dash white pepper
1 tablespoon lemon juice
3 tablespoons olive oil

1. Place tofu in blender with all other ingredients.
2. Blend at high speed until oil is incorporated and mayonnaise is creamy.

Tofu mayonnaise will keep in refrigerator about 2 weeks.

These not only make an excellent entree, but when put into whole wheat buns and topped with sliced tomato, lettuce, alfalfa sprouts, mayonnaise, and catsup, they also make delicious sandwiches.

Savory Sun Patties

½ pound dried chick-peas
1 cup hulled sunflower seeds
1 egg
1 tablespoon lemon juice
½ onion, chopped
1 small clove garlic, mashed
salt
dash cayenne
1 cup or more bread crumbs
3 tablespoons chopped parsley
whole wheat flour
salt
olive oil

1. Cook chick-peas according to basic directions (see pages 23–26). Drain, reserving broth.
2. Put into a blender, in batches, sunflower seeds,

chick-peas, egg, lemon juice, onion, garlic, salt, cayenne, and just enough reserved bean broth to blend ingredients. Blend a few seconds. It needn't be smooth. Pour into a bowl and add bread crumbs and parsley.

3. Form into 3-inch patties. Dust each with flour mixed with a dash of salt.

4. Fry in olive oil until golden brown on both sides. You may garnish with sprigs of parsley and lemon wedges. Our kids like them with catsup. Serves 4.

Cheese topped casseroles coming out of the oven steaming hot always look appealing. This tasty one has a tantalizing aroma as well.

Swiss Cheese and Lentil Casserole

½ pound lentils
3 tablespoons butter
1 large onion, chopped
1 cup coarsley chopped celery
1 cup diced carrots
2 cloves garlic, crushed
1 teaspoon oregano
½ teaspoon basil
¼ teaspoon thyme
1 cup brown rice
2 cups vegetable broth
salt
¼ teaspoon white pepper
6 ounces shredded Swiss cheese

1. Cook lentils according to basic directions (see pages 23–26). After lentils are cooked, drain, reserving 1 cup broth.

2. Melt butter in a 2½- to 3-quart saucepan. Add onion, celery, carrots, garlic, and herbs. Sauté until onion is transparent. Add rice and continue to sauté and stir until rice turns opaque.

3. Add reserved lentil broth, vegetable broth, salt, and

107

pepper. Bring to a boil, reduce heat to low, cover pan, and cook 40 to 45 minutes or until rice and vegetables are tender.

4. Combine rice mixture, lentils, and 4 ounces of the cheese in a 2½- to 3-quart casserole dish. Adjust seasonings.

5. Cover and bake at 350°F. for 25 minutes or until hot throughout.

6. Sprinkle top with remaining cheese and return to oven, uncovered, 3 or 4 minutes or until cheese has melted. Serve immediately to 4.

Garlic bread and a tossed salad go well with this casserole.

I love to cook this in late summer, when I have fresh vegetables growing and ready to be picked in the garden.

Summer Vegetables and Lentils

½ pound lentils
4 tablespoons olive oil
1 large onion, sliced
2 cups fresh green beans, cut in 1-inch lengths
1 large zucchini, sliced
1 small head cauliflower, broken into flowerettes
2 large tomatoes, peeled and chopped
1 cup vegetable broth
salt
dash white pepper
2 tablespoons chopped parsley
1 tablespoon chopped basil

1. Cook lentils according to basic directions (see pages 23–26) until tender but not too soft. Drain.

2. Heat olive oil in a large saucepan. Fry onion and green beans until onion is transparent. Add zucchini and cauliflower and stir-fry 5 minutes longer.

3. Add tomatoes, vegetable broth, salt, and pepper,

and cook until all vegetables are tender. Add drained lentils, parsley, and basil and cook until heated through. Serves 4.

We like this with whole wheat bread and a fresh fruit salad.

Simple and hearty is this recipe from Tennessee.

Tennessee Lentils

1 pound lentils
1 large onion, chopped
1½ cups diced carrots
1 cup water
1½ cups diced potatoes
2 cups broccoli or cauliflower—flowerettes quartered; stems peeled
  and sliced
2 bay leaves
1 teaspoon oregano
½ teaspoon thyme
salt
¼ teaspoon white pepper

1. Cook lentils, using 6 cups water, according to basic directions (see pages 23–26).

2. Cook onion and carrots in water for 5 minutes. Add potatoes and cook 3 minutes. Add broccoli, bay leaves, oregano, and thyme, and cook until all vegetables are tender but not falling apart.

3. Shortly before serving, combine the vegetables, lentils, salt, and pepper and cook 5 minutes. Serves 6 to 8.

It was suggested that this be served over rice with corn bread on the side.

A delicious and hearty stew is always welcome, but is especially so on a cold winter evening.

Lentil Stew with Mushrooms

1 pound lentils
3 tablespoons olive oil
1 large onion, chopped
1 large clove garlic, mashed
3 cups (¾ pound) mushrooms, halved or quartered, depending on
    size
5 carrots, cut in ½-inch discs
5 stalks celery, cut in ½-inch slices
2 turnips, cubed
2 potatoes, cubed
1 leek, cut in ½-inch slices
2 cups chopped tomatoes (fresh or canned)
salt
⅛ teaspoon white pepper
½ teaspoon Italian seasoning

1. Cook lentils according to basic directions (see pages 23–26). Drain, reserving broth.

2. In a large kettle, heat olive oil and sauté onion, garlic, and mushrooms until onion is lightly browned.

3. Add remaining ingredients, except lentils. Add 1 cup reserved lentil broth and bring to a boil. Reduce heat and cook gently until vegetables are tender.

4. Shortly before serving, add the lentils and remaining lentil broth and bring to a boil. Cook 5 minutes and serve with bulgur, brown rice, or whole wheat bread. Serves 6 to 8.

In this flavorful lentil dish, any greens—beet, turnip, mustard, dandelion greens, or Swiss chard—may be used.

Lentils with Vegetables and Egg Sauce

½ pound lentils
1 medium onion, chopped
1 clove garlic, mashed
2 tablespoons olive oil
2 carrots, halved or quartered lengthwise, then sliced
½ teaspoon oregano
10 ounces spinach (fresh or frozen)
2 eggs
1 tablespoon lemon juice
salt
⅛ teaspoon white pepper

1. Cook lentils according to basic directions (see pages 23–26). Drain, reserving broth.

2. In a large saucepan, sauté onion and garlic in the oil until onion is slightly browned.

3. Add carrots, oregano, and 1 cup of the reserved lentil broth. Simmer until carrots are tender.

4. Wash and cut spinach. Add it to the carrots and cook about 3 minutes or until spinach is cooked.

5. Beat eggs and lemon juice together in a small bowl. Set aside.

6. Shortly before serving, combine lentils and remaining lentil broth (not more than 1 cup) with the vegetables. Bring to a full boil and add salt, pepper, and egg sauce.

7. Remove pan from heat and stir lentils. Serve immediately to 3 or 4.

Serve with whole wheat toast or warmed whole wheat Arab pita bread.

A piquant sauce gives the lentils here a special flavor.

Sweet and Sour Lentils

½ pound dried lentils
3 vegetable bouillon cubes
½ cup water
⅓ cup apple cider
¼ cup apple cider vinegar
1½ tablespoons granulated fructose sugar
1 tablespoon blackstrap molasses
⅛ teaspoon ground cloves
2 bay leaves
1 tablespoon chopped scallions
dash cayenne
salt

1. Cook lentils according to basic directions (see pages 23–26), using 3 cups water.

2. In a small saucepan, dissolve 3 vegetable bouillon cubes in water. Add apple cider, vinegar, fructose, molasses, cloves, bay leaves, scallions, and cayenne. Boil 2 minutes.

3. Combine sauce with lentils. Add salt and cook until hot and bubbling. Serves 3 or 4.

Whole wheat bread or corn bread go well with the lentils, and a tossed salad adds a refreshing touch.

This is an excellent dish to prepare when you have masses of vegetables ripening in the garden.

Savory Stuffed Vegetables

1 cup dried lentils
1 cup brown rice
3 small zucchini (8 inches long)
3 yellow squash
3 large green peppers
6 tomatoes
⅔ cup olive oil
3 cloves garlic, halved
salt
¼ teaspoon cayenne
¼ cup finely chopped basil
½ cup finely chopped parsley
1 large egg, lightly beaten

1. Cook lentils according to basic directions (see pages 23–26). Drain and place in a large bowl.

2. Cook rice in double its volume of lightly salted water until tender and water is absorbed, 25 to 45 minutes. Combine with lentils.

3. Cut off a slice, about ½ inch, along the length of the zucchini and yellow squash. Scoop out centers, leaving ½-inch shells, making little boats. Reserve squash trimmings.

4. Cut peppers in half lengthwise. Remove seeds and membranes.

5. Steam squashes and peppers for about 8 minutes, or until tender but still retaining their shape. Drain.

6. Remove cores and a thin slice from the top of the tomatoes. Scoop out centers, leaving a ½-inch shell. Reserve pulp and juice. Salt tomatoes and turn upside down on paper towels to drain.

7. Heat ⅓ cup of the olive oil in a skillet. Brown garlic cloves. You may remove them.

8. Chop the reserved squash trimmings and fry in the hot oil.

9. Chop the reserved tomato pulp and add it and the

113

juice to the skillet. Add salt and cayenne and cook until squash is tender. Add basil and parsley, and pour contents from skillet into the bowl of rice and lentils. Add remaining olive oil and egg and mix thoroughly but gently. Adjust salt.

10. Fill vegetables with stuffing and place them side by side in an oiled baking dish. Cover and bake 30 to 40 minutes or until done.

11. Bake along with vegetables any remaining stuffing in an individual baking dish. Serve with Spanish tomato sauce if desired (see recipe page 101). Serves 8.

I like whole wheat bread to accompany this dish and a fresh fruit salad to follow.

These sandwiches taste great, look attractive, and can be made up in no time.

Open-Faced Bean Sandwiches

English muffin halves, toasted and buttered
prepared mustard
catsup
leftover baked beans, canned vegetarian beans, or canned baked
  beans
salt
white pepper
sliced tomatoes
cheddar cheese, sliced

1. On each muffin half spread a little mustard, some catsup, a thick layer of beans, salt, pepper, and a slice of tomato. Top with cheese.

2. Place sandwiches on a cookie sheet and bake in a 350°F. oven about 10 minutes or until cheese is bubbly and sandwich is heated through.

Beanburgers are delicious, satisfying, and easy to prepare. You will want to have them often.

Beanburgers

1 cup dried pinto beans
1 onion, chopped
2 tablespoons peanut oil
2 tablespoons bread crumbs
2 tablespoons chili sauce or catsup
½ teaspoon prepared mustard
salt
dash cayenne
cheddar cheese, sliced
4 6-inch loaves of whole wheat pita bread or 8 large whole wheat
  bread slices
alfalfa sprouts or lettuce

1. Cook beans according to basic directions (see pages 23–26). Drain, reserving some broth.

2. Sauté onion in peanut oil until golden. Add drained beans and mash in the pan. It is not necessary to have them smooth.

3. Add bread crumbs, chili sauce, mustard, salt, and cayenne.

4. Mix well and moisten with a little of the reserved bean broth if necessary.

5. Divide mixture into 4 parts. Form into large, flat burgers, and fry on one side, in a little oil, over medium heat until lightly browned.

6. Turn beanburgers over with a large spatula and place slices of cheese on top.

7. Lay pita bread flat and cut horizontally, separating the top of the loaves from the bottom. When beanburgers are done on the underside and cheese is soft, lift beanburgers onto the bottom halves of the pita bread. Sprinkle with a handful of alfalfa sprouts, or lettuce and place the other halves of the pita bread on top. Or make sandwiches on whole wheat bread. Serves 4.

Set out on the table mayonnaise, mustard, chili sauce, pickles, green onions, and sliced tomatoes.

115

EUROPE

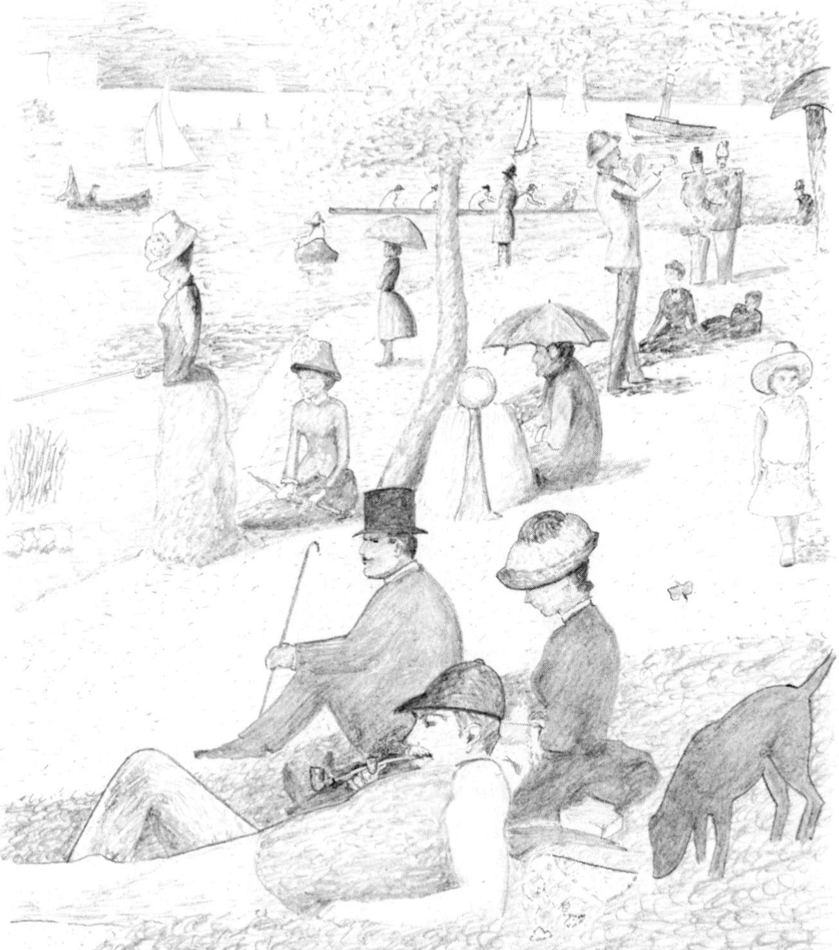

Europe

This nutritious dish is really flavorful, easy to prepare, and popular with my family.

Riso e Fagioli

(Rice and Beans Italian Style)

1 cup dried navy or pea beans
1½ cups brown rice, uncooked
¼ cup olive oil
3 cloves garlic, peeled and halved
¼ teaspoon crushed red pepper
1 pound (about 3) potatoes, peeled and diced
1 cup tomatoes, chopped
2 cups tomato puree
salt
1 tablespoon chopped fresh basil (or 1 teaspoon dried)
¼ cup chopped fresh parsley
⅓ cup grated Romano cheese

1. Cook beans according to basic directions (see pages 23–26). Drain, reserving ½ cup broth.
2. Cook rice in 3 cups lightly salted water until tender and water is absorbed.
3. Heat olive oil and brown garlic cloves. Add red pepper, and when pepper turns a shade darker, add potatoes.
4. Sauté potatoes 4 or 5 minutes and add tomatoes, tomato puree, reserved bean broth, salt, and basil. Let simmer until potatoes are tender. (Garlic pieces may be removed if desired.)
5. Add cooked beans, rice, and parsley, and cook until piping hot.
6. Pour into a serving bowl. Stir in ½ the cheese. Sprinkle remaining cheese on top. Serves 6.

I like a large salad of mixed greens with an oil and vinegar dressing to follow this.

117

I like to serve this attractive entree at lunch, but it is enjoyed at dinner as well.

Zucchini Boats

¾ cup dried navy beans
5 or 6 zucchini squash (7 to 9 inches long)
1 large onion, chopped
1 clove garlic, mashed
dash crushed red pepper
2 tablespoons olive oil
1 16-ounce can tomato sauce
salt
1 teaspoon Italian seasoning
4 cups fresh whole wheat bread cubes
¼ cup chopped parsley
grated Romano cheese

1. Cook beans according to basic directions (see pages 23–26). Drain.

2. Parboil whole zucchini for about 8 minutes. Drain and cool.

3. Sauté onion, garlic, and red pepper in olive oil until onion is transparent. Add tomato sauce, salt, and Italian seasoning. Simmer for 15 minutes.

4. Cut a slice, about ¼ inch deep, along the side of each squash. Hollow it out, leaving about ¼ inch shell for the boats.

5. Chop the zucchini trimmings and add to the sauce. Cook sauce until zucchini is thoroughly cooked. Add a little water if sauce becomes too thick. Adjust seasonings. Remove 1¼ cups of the sauce, reserve and keep hot.

6. Stir bread cubes, beans, and parsley into remaining sauce.

7. Fill zucchini boats with this stuffing and place in oiled baking dish.

8. Bake in a preheated 350°F. oven 40 to 45 minutes or until zucchini is thoroughly cooked. Spoon some of the reserved sauce over zucchini boats and sprinkle with Romano cheese. Pass the remaining sauce and additional cheese at the table.

This goes very well with brown rice or bulgur and a green salad. The stuffing can be used to fill parboiled green peppers or other vegetables which can be hollowed out and filled.

Of all the Italian dishes my mother has prepared over the years, this simple beans and greens combination remains one of my favorites. When she pulled out of the oven her freshly baked bread as an accompaniment, the meal was perfect.

Italian Beans and Greens

1 pound dried great northern beans
2 large bunches (or more) greens (dandelion, mustard, turnip, or rappini preferred)
⅔ cup olive oil
4 large cloves garlic, halved
⅛ to ¼ teaspoon crushed red pepper
½ cup peeled and chopped tomatoes
1 teaspoon oregano
salt

1. Cook beans according to basic directions (see pages 23–26).
2. Pick over greens, wash thoroughly, and cut into about 3-inch lengths. Blanch the greens in a large pot of boiling, lightly salted water. When water returns to the boil, drain greens and set aside. There should be at least 3 cups of blanched greens.
3. Heat olive oil in a saucepan. Add garlic cloves and brown on both sides. Add red pepper and remove pan from heat so that pepper will darken but not burn. Remove ½ the garlic-oil mixture and set aside.
4. In the remaining oil and garlic, cook tomatoes for 2 minutes. Add greens and salt, and cook until greens are tender.
5. Add reserved oil and garlic, along with oregano and salt, to cooked beans. Cook 5 to 10 minutes more to allow flavors to blend. (Garlic pieces may be removed if desired.) Serves 6 to 8.

119

Serve beans and greens with homemade or bakery whole wheat, Italian bread.

We always considered it a treat when my mother served this tasty dish to the family. She usually had fresh homemade bread to accompany it.

Italian Style Beans and Savoy Cabbage

½ pound great northern beans
⅓ cup olive oil
3 cloves garlic, halved
⅛ to ¼ teaspoon crushed red pepper
½ teaspoon oregano
1 head Savoy cabbage (about 8 inches across)—core, remove tough
   ribs, and cut in 2-inch chunks
salt

1. Cook beans according to basic directions (see pages 23–26). Drain, reserving broth.

2. In a 6-quart pan, heat olive oil over medium-high heat. Brown garlic pieces on both sides. Add red pepper and remove pan from heat when pepper becomes a shade darker. Add oregano.

3. Add cabbage and stir while frying for 2 minutes.

4. Add 2 cups of reserved bean broth. Cover pan and simmer about 10 minutes or until cabbage is tender.

5. Shortly before serving, garlic pieces may be removed if desired. Add beans and salt. Bring to a boil, reduce heat, and simmer 5 minutes to blend flavors.

This old Italian recipe has been in my family for generations. It is one of our favorite dishes.

Pasta e Fagioli

½ pound dried great northern beans
¼ cup olive oil
3 cloves garlic, halved
⅛ teaspoon crushed red pepper
1 cup heavy tomato puree
1 14-ounce can whole Italian plum tomatoes, chopped
salt
¼ cup chopped fresh parsley
1 tablespoon chopped fresh basil (or 1 teaspoon dried)
1 pound homemade noodles (½ × 2 inches), or small elbow macaroni
 or shells

1. Cook beans according to basic directions (see pages 23–26). Drain, reserving 1 cup of bean broth.
2. In a large saucepan, heat olive oil and sauté garlic pieces until browned. Add red pepper, sauté a few seconds and remove from heat so that pepper does not burn. Add tomato puree, tomatoes, salt, and the 1 cup of bean broth. Simmer a few minutes and remove garlic if desired. Add drained beans and simmer another few minutes to allow flavors to blend. Add parsley and basil. Sauce should not be too thick. Add a little water if necessary.
3. Cook pasta in 4 quarts of lightly salted, boiling water until tender but not overdone. Drain and put into serving bowl.
4. Pour ⅔ of beans and sauce over cooked pasta and mix thoroughly. Pour remaining beans and sauce evenly over top. Serves 4.

I like to pass freshly grated Romano cheese at the table.

Following the pasta e fagioli, we like a green salad. My favorite greens for this are romaine lettuce, arugula, endive, and tender, young dandelion leaves. Dress with olive oil and red wine vinegar, a touch of oregano, salt, and white pepper.

121

Pasta e Ceci

Follow the recipe for pasta e fagioli but substitute chick-peas for beans.

This old, family recipe is spicy and delicious.

Polenta con Fagioli

(Cornmeal Mush and Beans)

½ pound marrow beans
3 tablespoons plus ¼ cup olive oil
5 cloves garlic, halved
¼ teaspoon crushed red pepper
2 cups heavy tomato puree
4 cups water
3 teaspoons salt
2 tablespoons chopped parsley
1 tablespoon chopped sweet basil
1 cup cornmeal
2 or 3 dried red peppers (hot or sweet as desired)

1. Cook beans according to basic directions (see pages 23–26) until tender but not too soft. Drain.

2. Heat 3 tablespoons of the olive oil in a large saucepan. Brown 2 cloves of garlic in the oil and add the crushed red pepper. Take the pan off the heat so that the pepper does not burn.

3. When the oil cools slightly, add tomato puree, water, salt, parsley, and basil. Bring the sauce to a boil and simmer for 5 minutes. (Remove garlic pieces if you wish.) Add the beans to the sauce. Bring to second boil.

4. Very gradually, add the cornmeal to the sauce while stirring vigorously and constantly, so that the cornmeal will not be lumpy. Continue to cook and stir after the cornmeal has been added until the mixture is thick and the cornmeal does not have a raw taste. Cover the pan and leave it on the lowest possible heat for 20 to 30 minutes, stirring occasionally.

5. In a small saucepan, heat the remaining ¼ cup olive oil and add remaining 3 cloves of garlic. Fry garlic pieces until they are brown. Break dried peppers into several pieces and remove seeds. Add the pepper pieces to the hot oil, swirl them until they darken a little and become crispy. Do not burn them.

6. Put the polenta into a serving bowl and pour the hot oil with garlic and pepper over it. Serve the polenta with a little of the oil and a couple of pieces of pepper on each serving. (The garlic may be discarded.)

I like to accompany this with a large green salad with an Italian dressing. Fresh fruit and cheese make a pleasant ending.

This tasty dish is easy to prepare and one the whole family will enjoy.

Zucchini and Beans with Pasta

½ pound dried great northern beans
6 cups sliced zucchini squash
2 tablespoons olive oil
1 medium onion, chopped
1 large clove garlic, mashed
1 29-ounce can heavy tomato puree
¾ cup water
4 or 5 leaves chopped fresh basil (or ½ teaspoon dried)
salt
⅛ teaspoon crushed red papper
½ cup chopped fresh parsley
1 pound elbow macaroni
2 rounded tablespoons grated Romano cheese

1. Cook beans according to basic directions (see pages 23–26). Drain, reserving ¾ cup of the broth.

2. Sauté zucchini in 1 tablespoon of the olive oil, in a large saucepan, until lightly browned. Remove from pan and reserve.

3. In the same pan, cook onion and garlic in remaining oil until onion is very soft.

4. Add reserved zucchini, tomato puree, water, the ¾ cup reserved bean broth, basil, salt, and pepper. Bring to a boil, reduce heat, and simmer for 10 minutes.

5. Add drained beans and parsley and cook an additional 5 minutes to allow flavors to blend. Add water if too thick and adjust seasoning.

6. Cook macaroni in lots of boiling, lightly salted water until done but not overcooked. Drain and put into serving bowl.

7. Spoon ¾ of the vegetable-bean sauce plus ½ the cheese over the macaroni. Mix well. Pour remaining sauce over macaroni and sprinkle remaining cheese on top. Serves 4 to 6.

A crisp green salad with an oil and vinegar dressing is nice following the pasta dish. Some fresh fruit and cheese might top it off.

The combination of celery and cauliflower gives this dish an excellent flavor.

Beans, Celery, and Cauliflower

½ pound great northern beans
¼ cup olive oil
3 cloves garlic, peeled and halved
⅛ teaspoon crushed red pepper
4 cups celery stalks and leaves, cut in ½-inch pieces
1 head cauliflower cut into flowerettes
2 cups cooked rice
1 teaspoon oregano
salt

1. Cook beans according to basic directions (see pages 23–26). Drain and reserve broth.

2. Heat olive oil in large saucepan. Cook garlic in oil until lightly browned.

3. Add pepper and celery and sauté for 5 minutes. Add cauliflower and continue to sauté another 5 minutes.

4. Pour in reserved bean broth, cover pan, and simmer until vegetables are tender. (You may remove garlic pieces at this time.)

5. Add beans, rice, oregano, and salt. Add water if necessary to keep dish moist. Simmer for 10 minutes to allow flavors to blend. Serves 4.

Italian bread and a tomato and lettuce salad go well with this.

The great northern beans blend very well in this creamy rice concoction, and the fresh mushrooms and peas are an attractive addition.

Risotto con Fagioli

(Italian Rice with Beans)

½ pound great northern beans
3 tablespoons butter
3 tablespoons olive oil
1 large onion, chopped
1 clove garlic, mashed
1½ cups short-grain Italian rice (Arborio)
6 cups well-seasoned vegetable broth
½ to 1 teaspoon saffron (optional)
½ pound fresh mushrooms, quartered and sautéd in butter
1 cup lightly cooked peas
¼ cup grated Parmesan cheese

1. Cook beans according to basic directions (see pages 23–26). Drain.

2. Heat butter and olive oil in a large, heavy saucepan and sauté onion and garlic until cooked but not browned.

3. Add rice and stir well until the grains turn opaque—about 2 to 3 minutes.

4. Bring vegetable broth to a boil. Add 2 cups of the broth to the rice and cook over medium heat uncovered. The rice will absorb the liquid. Stir occasionally.

5. As the liquid is absorbed, continue adding broth, 1 cup at a time, stirring frequently, and allowing the liquid to be absorbed before adding more.

6. Steep the saffron in the last cup of broth before adding it to the rice.

7. When the rice has absorbed all the broth, is tender, and has a creamy consistency, gently stir in the beans, sautéd mushrooms, peas, and Parmesan cheese. Cover pan and keep on lowest possible heat for 5 minutes.

8. Put in a serving bowl or platter and sprinkle additional Parmesan cheese over top. More cheese may be passed at the table. Serves 6.

I like a large tossed salad with this meal, and I like it served along side the risotto instead of afterward.

This layered casserole, featuring a blending of several different flavors and textures, is one of my favorite eggplant preparations.

Italian Layered Eggplant Casserole

½ pound dried baby lima beans
3 medium eggplants, peeled and sliced about ½ inch thick
olive oil for broiling eggplant, plus ¼ cup olive oil
3 green peppers, seeded and sliced
1 large onion, chopped
2 cloves garlic, mashed
¼ teaspoon crushed red pepper
salt
1 cup chopped tomatoes
1 28-ounce can tomato puree
¼ teaspoon Italian seasoning
1 tablespoon chopped fresh basil (or ½ teaspoon dried)
1 tablespoon chopped fresh parsley
½ pound provolone cheese, sliced
½ cup grated Romano cheese

1. Cook beans according to basic directions (see pages 23–26). Drain well.

2. Brush olive oil on both sides of eggplant slices and broil on both sides until lightly browned. Set aside.

3. In a large saucepan, heat ¼ cup olive oil and fry green peppers. Remove peppers and reserve. In the same oil, fry onion, garlic, and crushed red pepper until onion is lightly browned.

4. Remove about 1 tablespoon of the oil from the saucepan and stir it, along with a little salt, into the drained beans.

5. To the saucepan, add tomatoes, tomato puree, Italian seasoning, basil, parsley, and salt. Let sauce simmer for 10 minutes.

6. To assemble, put a little sauce in the bottom of a 3-quart casserole dish. Layer ⅓ of the eggplant slices, ⅓ of the beans, ⅓ of the green pepper slices, and ⅓ of the provolone cheese slices, all distributed evenly. Spoon a layer of tomato sauce over the provolone cheese and sprinkle with about ⅓ of the Romano cheese.

7. Make another layer of eggplant, beans, green pepper, provolone, tomato sauce, and Romano cheese, and then a third layer using remaining ingredients in the same order.

8. Cover and bake in a preheated 350°F. oven about 30 or 35 minutes or until bubbling and cooked through. Serves 4 to 6.

Serve with whole wheat Italian bread and a mixed greens salad with Italian dressing.

Lima beans are particularly delicious in this tomato sauce made in the style of Naples.

Lima Beans alla Napoletana

1 pound dried lima beans
½ small onion, chopped
2 cloves garlic, halved
⅛ to ¼ teaspoon crushed red pepper
3 tablespoons olive oil
2 cups tomato puree and chopped whole tomatoes combined
½ cup water
1 tablespoon chopped fresh basil (or 1 teaspoon dried)
3 rounded tablespoons chopped fresh parsley
salt
1 cup grated Parmesan cheese

1. Cook beans according to basic directions (see pages 23–26). Drain, reserving 1 cup bean broth.

2. In a large saucepan, sauté onion, garlic pieces, and pepper in oil until onion and garlic are lightly browned.

3. Add tomato mixture, reserved bean broth, water, basil, parsley, and salt. Simmer sauce 15 minutes. (Garlic pieces may be removed if desired.)

4. Shortly before serving, add lima beans to sauce and simmer 5 to 10 minutes.

5. Pour into a serving dish and top with some of the cheese. Pass remaining cheese at the table. Serves 6 to 8.

Serve with hot buttered noodles. Sprinkle some of the Parmesan over the noodles. A fresh green salad with a light oil and vinegar dressing is a good accompaniment.

The possibilities for legume and pasta combinations are end-less. This dish, with cauliflower and olives, has a uniquely delicious flavor.

Legumi e Pasta

½ pound dried chick-peas
3 tablespoons olive oil
2 cloves garlic, halved
⅛ teaspoon crushed red pepper
1 small head of cauliflower, cut into small flowerettes, or 1 10-ounce
    package frozen cauliflower, thawed
3 cups chopped tomatoes
1 tablespoon wine vinegar
salt
1 teaspoon chopped fresh basil (or ½ teaspoon dried)
½ can black olives, drained and halved
¼ cup chopped parsley
1 pound small shell or elbow macaroni
2 rounded tablespoons grated Romano cheese

1. Cook chick-peas according to basic directions (see pages 23–26). Drain.

2. Heat olive oil and sauté garlic pieces until they are brown. Add red pepper and cauliflower and sauté for 3 minutes.

3. Add tomatoes, vinegar, salt, basil, and olives. Bring to a boil, reduce heat, and simmer until cauliflower is tender. (Garlic pieces may be removed if desired.)

4. Add parsley and chick-peas to sauce and simmer about 5 minutes. Adjust seasonings.

5. Boil macaroni in lightly salted water until tender. Drain.

6. Combine macaroni with ¾ of the sauce and vegetables in a serving bowl. Top with remaining sauce and vegetables. Sprinkle top with Romano cheese. Serves 4 to 6.

I like to serve a green salad with an Italian dressing following the pasta dish.

If this is put into an attractive casserole dish, it can go from oven to table, looking tempting, steaming hot, with the melted cheese on top.

Legumes Italiano

1 cup Roman or cranberry beans
2 large cloves garlic, mashed
1 large onion, sliced
¼ cup olive oil
3 green peppers, sliced
2 medium eggplants, peeled, cubed, and lightly salted
1 medium zucchini squash, sliced
1 15½-ounce can whole tomatoes, coarsely chopped
salt
¼ teaspoon crushed red pepper
¼ teaspoon Italian seasoning
¼ teaspoon oregano
1 teaspoon chopped fresh basil (or ½ teaspoon dried)
¼ cup chopped fresh parsley
¼ cup grated Parmesan cheese
¼ pound mozzarella cheese, sliced

1. Cook beans according to basic directions (see pages 23–26). Drain.

2. Sauté garlic and onion in olive oil until onion is transparent.

3. Add pepper slices and fry until they are limp.

4. Add eggplant cubes and zucchini and continue to fry while stirring, about 5 minutes.

5. Add tomatoes, with their juice.

6. Add the seasonings and herbs and simmer until all vegetables are cooked.

7. Add drained beans and let mixture come to the boil.

8. Pour into a large, shallow casserole dish, sprinkle Parmesan cheese over vegetables and place slices of mozzarella cheese on top.

9. Bake at 350°F. oven about 15 minutes or until bubbling and cheese is slightly browned. Serves 6.

Serve with whole wheat Italian bread and a tossed salad with an oil and vinegar dressing.

Greens and beans always make a winning combination. This unusual treatment is no exception. Spinach, beet greens, or other greens may be used in place of the Swiss chard.

Swiss Chard and Black-Eyed Peas

1 pound dried black-eyed peas
2 pounds Swiss chard
4 tablespoons olive oil
2 onions, chopped
2 cloves garlic, mashed
¼ teaspoon crushed red pepper
¼ teaspoon allspice
½ cup raisins
1 cup black olives, pitted and halved
salt

1. Cook black-eyed peas according to basic directions (see pages 23–26). Drain and reserve 1 cup broth.

2. Wash and cut Swiss chard in 3-inch pieces and set aside.

3. In a large saucepan, heat olive oil and sauté onions and garlic, with red pepper and allspice, until onion is lightly browned.

4. Add 1 cup reserved black-eyed pea broth, raisins, and Swiss chard. Bring to a boil, reduce heat, and simmer a few minutes until Swiss chard is cooked.

5. Add olives, black-eyed peas, and salt. Bring to a boil again, lower heat, and simmer 5 minutes to allow flavors to blend. Serves 6 to 8.

Homemade or bakery whole wheat bread is especially good with this. Sliced beets make a pleasant salad to follow, and rice pudding an appropriate dessert.

Black-eyed peas and artichoke hearts give a distinctively deli-cious flavor to the sauce, which combines well with the spaghetti.

Spaghetti, Black-Eyed Peas, and Artichoke Hearts

½ pound dried black-eyed peas
¼ cup olive oil
2 cloves garlic, halved
⅛ teaspoon crushed red pepper
½ cup chopped scallions
1 10-ounce package frozen artichoke hearts, quartered
1 cup black olives, halved
salt
¼ cup chopped parsley
1 pound spaghetti, broken into 1-inch lengths
2 rounded tablespoons grated Parmesan cheese

1. Cook black-eyed peas according to basic directions (see pages 23–26). Drain, reserving broth.

2. Heat olive oil in large saucepan and brown garlic pieces. Add pepper, scallions, and artichoke hearts and sauté for 4 or 5 minutes. (Garlic pieces may be removed if desired.)

3. Add olives, 2 to 2½ cups reserved bean broth, and salt. Bring to a boil, reduce heat, and simmer 5 minutes. Add black-eyed peas and parsley.

4. Cook spaghetti, al dente, drain, and put into serving bowl. Spoon ½ of the sauce and ½ of the cheese over the spaghetti. Mix well. Spoon remaining sauce and cheese over spaghetti. Serves 4.

A tossed salad with an oil and vinegar dressing may be served following this. Fresh fruit and cheese may be offered to complete the meal.

Lentil balls are unlike meatballs, but they are delicious with this tomato sauce.

Spaghetti and Lentil Balls

½ pound dried lentils
⅓ cup wheat germ
1 cup fresh whole wheat bread crumbs
salt
⅛ teaspoon white pepper
¼ cup grated Romano cheese
1 large egg
3 cloves garlic, mashed
¼ cup chopped parsley
olive oil for frying lentil balls
1 cup canned Italian plum tomatoes, chopped
2 cups heavy tomato puree
1 cup water
1 tablespoon chopped fresh basil (or 1 teaspoon dried)
⅛ teaspoon crushed red pepper
1 pound spaghetti

1. Cook lentils according to basic directions (see pages 23–26) and drain well.

2. Mash lentils in a large bowl.

3. Add wheat germ, bread crumbs, salt, pepper, 1 rounded tablespoon of the cheese, egg, ½ of the mashed garlic, and ½ of the chopped parsley. Mix well and adjust seasonings.

4. In a heavy pan, heat enough olive oil to cover the bottom of the pan. Form balls by rolling a rounded table-spoon of lentil mixture in the palms of your hands. Wet your palms with a little water, and the mixture will not stick to your hands.

5. Set lentil balls in the hot oil and fry them, one layer at a time, until they are browned on all sides. Remove them from the pan and keep them warm in the oven.

6. Combine in the pan, tomatoes, tomato puree, water, remaining mashed garlic, basil, salt, and red pepper. Bring to a boil, scraping loose all the browned particles. Reduce heat and simmer 30 minutes. Add remaining pars-ley and additional water if sauce is too thick. Adjust salt and continue to simmer.

7. Cook spaghetti al dente, drain, and put into serving bowl. Spoon some sauce over the spaghetti and sprinkle with a rounded tablespoon of the Romano cheese. Mix thoroughly. Spoon more sauce over spaghetti and sprinkle with remaining cheese.

8. Spoon some sauce over lentil balls and pass the rest at the table, along with additional grated cheese. Makes about 2 dozen balls.

A green salad with an oil and vinegar dressing should follow.

Mushrooms, garlic, butter, and cream set the style for this rich French delight.

Lima Beans a la Mode Paris

1 pound dried baby lima beans
½ pound mushrooms, sliced
2 tablespoons butter
1 onion, chopped
1 clove garlic, crushed
1 egg yolk, beaten
½ cup cream
salt
dash white pepper

1. Cook lima beans according to basic directions (see pages 23–26). Drain, reserving 1 cup of the broth.

2. Sauté mushrooms in 1 tablespoon of the butter. Remove from skillet and reserve.

3. Add remaining butter and cook the onion and garlic until soft but not brown. Add sautéd mushrooms, beans, and reserved bean broth and bring to a boil. Reduce heat and simmer 10 minutes.

4. Combine egg yolk and cream and add to the bean mixture. Simmer 5 minutes but do not boil. Add salt and pepper and serve immediately to 6 or 8.

This goes well with noodles, bulgur, or whole wheat toast and asparagus or another green vegetable.

I enjoy preparing this gourmet dish mostly because I like the fun of turning the crepes by flipping them high in the air with the crepe pan. It is not difficult. Shake the pan back and forth to loosen the crepe. Then, in one jerk, fling the pan up away from you. The crepe will go flying, flip over, and return to the pan if you hold the pan directly under the descending crepe. Give it a try! Then enjoy the exquisite delicacy of texture and flavor.

Baby Lima Filled Crepes

1 cup dried baby lima beans
Crepes (12 to 14):
  2 cups milk
  4 eggs
  ½ teaspoon salt
  2 cups whole wheat pastry flour
  4 tablespoons melted butter
¾ pound fresh spinach (or 1 10-ounce package frozen)
salt
⅛ teaspoon white pepper
3 tablespoons butter
½ pound fresh mushrooms, sliced
2 tablespoons minced green onion
Cheese sauce:
  4 tablespoons butter
  5 tablespoons whole wheat flour
  3½ cups scalded milk
  ½ teaspoon salt
  dash white pepper
  dash nutmeg
  1 egg, beaten
  3 ounces Swiss cheese, shredded
¼ pound Swiss cheese, sliced

1. Cook lima beans according to basic directions (see pages 23–26). Drain.

2. While beans are resting, prepare batter for crepes: Place all batter ingredients in an electric blender and blend at high speed, about 1 minute. Scrape down the sides of the blender jar with a rubber spatula to remove any flour that may have adhered to the jar. Blend another few seconds. Refrigerate for 1 hour or longer.

Heat a 7-inch crepe pan or skillet and brush lightly with

oil. Pour a scant ¼ cup of batter into pan and tilt pan all around to evenly cover the bottom of the pan. Cook about 1 minute, or peek under an edge and turn when lightly browned. The crepe can be turned with a spatula, your fingers, or by a flip of the pan. Cook the other side about 30 seconds or until it shows some brown spots. Stack crepes on a plate, spotty side up, and cover with a towel until ready to fill.

3. Cook spinach in a small amount of water, drain well, and chop. Add to beans with a little salt and pepper.

4. Heat 3 tablespoons butter in a skillet and sauté mushrooms and onion until they are lightly browned.

5. Prepare cheese sauce: Melt 4 tablespoons butter in a saucepan. Add flour and cook, stirring, 2 or 3 minutes over medium heat. Beat in the milk and seasonings with a wire whisk and bring to a boil. Boil 1 minute while stirring. Blend into the egg, gradually, 2 tablespoons of the sauce. Then add egg mixture to the sauce. Add shredded Swiss cheese and stir until cheese melts. Remove from heat.

6. To assemble, spread a spoonful of the bean-spinach mixture below the center of the crepe. Place 6 slices of sautéd mushrooms, evenly distributed, over beans and top with sliced Swiss cheese. Roll into cylindrical shape and place in shallow, buttered baking dish, seam side down. Continue to fill crepes, and place them close together in the dish.

7. Spoon sauce over crepes to cover. Bake in upper half of a preheated 400°F. oven until bubbling and lightly browned, about 20 minutes. Serve with remaining sauce. Makes 12 to 14 filled crepes.

Colorful peas and carrots go well with this. Complete the meal with stewed pears in a lightly spiced syrup using honey, water, cinnamon, cloves, and cardamom.

The addition of beans makes this quiche more satisfying and less rich than most.

Bean and Spinach Quiche

½ small onion, finely chopped
2 tablespoons butter
1 cup cooked and drained white beans
1 bunch fresh spinach, washed, chopped, and steamed until wilted,
   or 1 10-ounce package chopped, frozen spinach, thawed and
   drained
salt
dash white pepper
dash nutmeg
4 eggs, lightly beaten
1¾ cups milk
pastry for a one-crust 9-inch pie (preferably whole wheat)
2 tablespoons grated Parmesan cheese
3 ounces Gruyère or Swiss cheese, sliced and cut into strips

1. Sauté onion in butter until soft and yellow. Add beans and mash slightly with onion. Add spinach and seasonings to beans. Blend the eggs and milk and gradually combine with the bean-spinach mixture.

2. Preheat oven to 450°F.

3. Line a 9-inch pie plate with pastry. Make a high, fluted edge, prick the bottom and sides with a fork, and bake 5 minutes.

4. Sprinkle the cheeses over the bottom of the partly baked pastry. Pour the bean and egg mixture over the cheese.

5. Bake the quiche for 15 minutes. Reduce oven temperature to 350°F. and bake another 10 to 15 minutes or until a knife inserted 2 inches from the pastry edge comes out clean. Serves 6 to 8.

Serve immediately as a first or main course. This quiche is also good chilled. I like to take it along on picnics.

This is a dish with a deep red color and a tantalizing aroma.

Feves Rouges aux Champignons

(Red Beans with Mushrooms)

1 pound dried red kidney beans
¾ pound fresh mushrooms, thickly sliced
2 tablespoons butter
2 tablespoons olive oil
1 large onion, chopped
2 tablespoons finely chopped shallots or 2 cloves garlic, mashed
2 carrots, scraped and thinly sliced
12 small whole onions, peeled
½ cup cream
¼ teaspoon thyme
salt
⅛ teaspoon white pepper
1 tablespoon chopped parsley

1. Cook beans according to basic directions (see pages 23–26). Drain, reserving bean broth.

2. In a large skillet, sauté mushrooms in the butter over a moderately high heat. Remove from skillet and reserve.

3. Add olive oil to skillet and sauté chopped onion and shallots or garlic until lightly browned.

4. In a large saucepan, cook carrots and small onions in very little water until tender. Add beans and about 1 cup of reserved bean broth, mushrooms, onions, shallots, cream, thyme, salt, and pepper.

5. Bring to a boil. Reduce heat and simmer about 10 minutes uncovered.

6. Add parsley, and additional bean broth if it becomes too thick. Serves 6 to 8.

Serve with lots of crusty whole wheat bread and a green salad with an oil and vinegar dressing that has a touch of powdered mustard in it.

This famous Greek casserole, usually made with meat, is equally appetizing with beans. It can be made ahead and reheated before serving. It is especially nice for buffets.

Bean Moussaka

1 pound great northern beans
4 medium-large eggplants
¼ cup olive oil
3 large onions, chopped
2 cloves garlic, mashed
1½ cups tomato puree
½ teaspoon cinnamon
pinch cloves
salt
¼ teaspoon white pepper
½ cup chopped fresh parsley
¼ pound butter
8 tablespoons whole wheat flour
4 cups scalded milk
1½ cups ricotta cheese
4 eggs, beaten
salt
¼ teaspoon nutmeg
¾ cup grated Romano cheese

1. Cook beans according to basic directions (see pages 23–26). Drain, reserving 1 cup of bean broth.

2. Peel and slice eggplants about ½ inch thick. Salt and place in layers on a plate. Place another plate on top of eggplant slices with a heavy weight on it. This helps to extract excess water from eggplant.

3. Heat olive oil and cook onions and garlic until golden. Add tomato puree and reserved bean broth, cinnamon, cloves, salt, and pepper. Cook until onions are very soft.

4. Add drained beans and parsley and cook over low heat until beans are heated through.

5. Melt butter in a saucepan to make bechamel sauce. Blend in the flour, stirring for 3 minutes over medium heat. Pour in the hot milk and beat with a wire whisk until sauce comes to a boil and is smooth.

140

6. Remove from heat, cool slightly, and stir in the ricotta, eggs, salt, and nutmeg.

7. Drain eggplant slices and pat dry with paper towels. Fry in olive oil until lightly browned or brush with olive oil and brown on both sides under broiler.

8. Assemble casserole: Oil an 11 × 16 × 2½-inch pan. Arrange a layer of eggplant on the bottom, using about ½ of the eggplant slices. Spoon in the bean mixture and sprinkle with ½ the Romano cheese. Place remaining eggplant over beans and pour white sauce over eggplant. Sprinkle with remaining Romano cheese and bake in 350°F. oven about 1 hour or until top is lightly browned.

9. Cut into squares and serve to 8 or more.

A piquant Mediterranean dish; satisfying and delicious.

Pintos and Prunes

1 cup dried pinto beans
¼ cup olive oil
1 large onion, chopped
1 clove garlic, mashed
2 cups fresh or canned tomatoes, peeled and chopped
¾ cup prunes, pitted and chopped
2 tablespoons vinegar
¼ cup apple juice
⅛ teaspoon cinnamon
dash cloves
dash nutmeg
2 bay leaves
salt
⅛ teaspoon white pepper
½ lemon, sliced

1. Cook beans according to basic directions (see pages 23–26). Drain, reserving a little broth.

2. Heat olive oil in a large skillet or saucepan. Lightly brown onion and garlic. Add all ingredients except beans and lemon slices and simmer for 20 to 30 minutes or until onion and prunes are well cooked.

3. Add drained beans and a little bean broth to thin the sauce if necessary. Add lemon slices and cook until very hot. Serve over noodles or rice to 3 or 4.

This Athenian treatment of chick-peas produces a meal worthy of the Gods.

Grecian Chick-Pea Stew

½ pound dried chick-peas
3 tablespoons olive oil
8 small onions
1½ cups sliced carrots
½ pound mushrooms, halved or quartered
1 2-inch cinnamon stick, broken in half
4 cloves
2 cups chopped Italian plum tomatoes
salt
½ teaspoon allspice
¼ teaspoon thyme
dash cayenne pepper
¼ cup chopped parsley
10 Greek black olives

1. Cook chick-peas according to basic directions (see pages 23–26). Drain.
2. In a stew pot, heat olive oil and brown onions, carrots, and mushrooms with cinnamon stick and cloves. When vegetables are lightly browned add tomatoes, salt, allspice, thyme, and cayenne. Simmer until carrots and onions are tender.
3. Add ½ of the parsley, then olives, and chick-peas to the pot. Simmer 10 minutes to allow flavors to blend. Pour into serving bowl and sprinkle remaining parsley over top. Serve with bulgur or brown rice. Serves 4.
A pleasant beginning to this meal would be a Greek salad with feta cheese, served with a good brown bread. An appropriate ending would be fresh figs with cream, or fresh fruit in season.

Pastitsio, a mass of steaming noodles covered with a golden brown topping, is as attractive in taste as in appearance. It cuts into squares for easy serving.

Pastitsio

(Greek Macaroni and Lentil Casserole)

1 cup dried lentils
6 tablespoons butter
⅓ cup whole wheat flour
4⅔ cups scalded milk
5 eggs
salt
dash white pepper
¼ cup olive oil
1 large onion, chopped
1 large clove garlic, crushed
1 cup tomatoes, chopped
2 tablespoons tomato paste
⅛ teaspoon cayenne
½ teaspoon thyme
1 teaspoon oregano
2 tablespoons chopped fresh parsley
1 pound macaroni (mostaccioli, ziti, or elbows)
½ cup grated Parmesan cheese
¼ cup grated Romano cheese

1. Cook lentils according to basic directions (see pages 23–26). Drain.

2. Make bechamel sauce: Melt butter in saucepan over medium heat. Stir in flour and cook, stirring constantly, for a few minutes. It should be bubbling but not brown. Pour in 4 cups of the hot milk, all at once while stirring vigorously with a whisk. Continue to stir until sauce boils, thickens, and is smooth.

3. Beat two of the eggs in a bowl and pour some of the sauce over them while beating. Pour the egg mixture into the bechamel sauce. Add salt and pepper and stir.

4. Remove 1⅓ cups of the sauce from saucepan and thin it with the remaining ⅔ cup milk. Set thin and thick sauces aside.

5. Heat olive oil in a large skillet. Fry the onion and garlic until slightly browned. Add tomatoes, tomato paste, salt, cayenne, thyme, and oregano. Cook for 10 minutes.

Add the cooked lentils and the parsley and cook another 5 minutes. Set aside.

6. Boil macaroni in lightly salted water until tender but not too soft. Drain in colander and put back in pan.

7. Beat remaining 3 eggs. Combine eggs, Parmesan cheese, the thin sauce, and the macaroni. Mix thoroughly.

8. Spread ½ the macaroni evenly in a large, buttered baking dish. Layer it with the lentil mixture and then cover with remaining macaroni. Spread the thick sauce over the macaroni and sprinkle with Romano cheese.

9. Bake in 350°F. oven for 30 to 45 minutes or until bubbling. Serves 6 or more.

To be enjoyed on St. Patrick's Day, or any other day, with great pleasure.

Irish Bean Stew

½ pound dried great northern beans
2 tablespoons vegetable oil
1 large onion, chopped
3 potatoes, cut in large cubes
3 carrots, sliced
½ teaspoon caraway seeds
4 cups cabbage, cut in chunks
1 cup peas
salt
dash white pepper

1. Cook beans according to basic directions (see pages 23–26). Drain, reserving broth.

2. Heat oil and sauté onion, potatoes, and carrots until lightly browned. Add caraway seeds and fry for 1 minute.

3. Add reserved bean broth and simmer until carrots are almost done.

4. Add cabbage and peas and cook 10 minutes longer.

5. Add beans, salt, and pepper. Cook 5 minutes. Adjust seasoning if necessary. Serves 4.

This dish goes nicely with Irish soda bread or hot corn bread. A warm fruit compote completes the meal.

These unusual pancakes have a surprisingly good flavor.

Heidelberg Bean Pancakes

¾ pound dried navy or pea beans
2 eggs, beaten
¼ cup whole wheat flour
¼ teaspoon baking powder
½ cup finely chopped onion
2 tablespoons chopped parsley
¼ teaspoon caraway seeds
salt
⅛ teaspoon white pepper
oil for frying

1. Cook beans according to basic directions (see pages 23–26). Drain.
2. Mash beans and combine with eggs, flour, baking powder, onion, parsley, caraway seeds, salt, and pepper. Mix thoroughly.
3. Drop by large spoonfuls (about ¼ cup) bean mixture into a little hot oil in a large frying pan. Fry pancakes on both sides until browned. Serves 6.

I like to serve these with German-style red cabbage and apple sauce. Pumpernickel bread goes well with this too.

The piquant flavors of sauerkraut, paprika, and sour cream complement the delicate beans.

Hungarian Limas

1 pound dried baby lima beans
1 large onion, finely chopped
2 tablespoons peanut oil
1½ quarts sauerkraut
1 cup heavy tomato puree
1 tablespoon paprika
salt
½ cup sour cream

1. Cook beans according to basic directions (see pages 23–26).

145

2. In a large saucepan, sauté onion in oil until lightly browned. Add sauerkraut and sauté 5 minutes. Add tomato puree, paprika, and salt. Simmer 45 minutes.

3. Add beans with the bean broth and mix gently but thoroughly. Simmer 10 minutes. Stir in sour cream and serve to 6.

Serve with rye bread, boiled potatoes, carrots cooked tender-crisp, and a fruit salad.

The Spanish brought the lima bean to Europe and featured it in their unique cuisine. Here is a tasty preparation from Barcelona.

Barcelona Limas

1 pound dried baby lima beans
1 large onion, chopped
2 green peppers, chopped
1 tablespoon olive oil
2 cups peeled and chopped tomatoes
¼ teaspoon cayenne
½ teaspoon oregano
¼ teaspoon ground cumin
salt
1½ cups grated cheddar cheese (reserve ½ cup)

1. Cook beans according to basic directions (see pages 23–26) and drain.

2. Sauté onion and green peppers in oil until soft.

3. Combine beans with all ingredients except ½ cup of the cheese.

4. Pour into a shallow baking dish and bake, uncovered, at 350°F. for about 30 minutes or until bubbling.

5. Sprinkle remaining cheese on top and return to the oven for a few minutes or until cheese melts. Serves 6.

This is nice with corn bread and a tossed salad.

This tasty black-eyed peas preparation is topped with whole eggs.

Portuguese Black-Eyed Peas

½ pound dried black-eyed peas
2 tablespoons olive oil
1 large onion, chopped
½ cup vegetable broth (may be made with vegetable bouillon cube)
2 tablespoons chopped fresh parsley
2 tablespoons chopped fresh coriander (optional)
¼ teaspoon liquid fructose sugar
salt
⅛ teaspoon cayenne
10 ounces cooked spinach
4 large eggs

1. Cook black-eyed peas according to basic directions (see pages 23–26). Drain, reserving ½ cup bean broth.

2. In a large skillet, heat olive oil and sauté onion until golden. Pour in vegetable broth and cook until onion is thoroughly done.

3. Add parsley, coriander, fructose, salt, cayenne, black-eyed peas, the ½ cup reserved bean broth, and the spinach. Stir well and bring to the boil.

4. With a large spoon, make 4 indentations in bean mixture in skillet. Break the eggs and place one in each indentation. Sprinkle a little salt on each egg. Cover skillet and cook 4 or 5 minutes or until eggs are set. Serve immediately to 4.

With this, I like whole wheat bread and a salad to follow.

Creamy, buttery, delicate, and delicious—this is a gourmet delight!

Scandinavian Lentil Puree

1 pound lentils
4 small (2 to 2½ cups) potatoes, peeled and diced
4 tablespoons butter
salt
⅛ teaspoon white pepper
½ cup heavy cream
chopped chives

1. Cook lentils according to basic directions (see pages 23–26) until they are soft.
2. Boil potatoes in lightly salted water until they are tender and drain.
3. Put lentils with their broth and the potatoes through the blender, in batches, to make a light puree.
4. Heat puree in a heavy saucepan, stirring occasionally, so it does not stick. Add butter, salt, pepper, and cream. Do not boil. Serve when it is very hot and top with chopped chives. Serves 6.

With this, I serve a hot green or yellow vegetable, dark pumpernickel bread, and a fruit compote.

LATIN AMERICA

Latin America

This casserole is a favorite of ours, one that I enjoy serving to family and guests. It is easy to prepare, it has an exciting flavor, and it looks attractive.

Mexican Casserole

1 pound dried red kidney beans
2 onions, chopped
1 clove garlic, mashed
1 tablespoon peanut oil
1 16-ounce can whole tomatoes, coarsely chopped
1 16-ounce can tomato sauce
2 rounded tablespoons chili powder
¼ teaspoon ground cumin
salt
1 10-ounce package frozen corn kernels
1 can pitted ripe olives, drained and halved
¼ teaspoon hot pepper sauce (or to taste)
1 dozen corn tortillas
6 scallions, chopped
¾ pound grated sharp cheddar cheese

1. Cook beans according to basic directions (see pages 23–26).

2. Sauté onions and garlic in peanut oil until lightly browned. Add tomatoes, tomato sauce, and seasonings.

3. Cook 10 minutes, add the beans with the bean broth, corn, olives, and hot pepper sauce. Cook until heated through. Adjust seasonings. Skim and reserve 1 cup of the thinner top of the bean mixture for sauce to pass at the table.

4. Line an oiled, 3½- or 4-quart casserole dish with tortillas. Spoon over them a thick layer (about 1 inch) of bean mixture, and sprinkle a few scallions on the beans. Scatter some cheese evenly over top. Reserve 1 cup of the cheese and some scallions for use later.

5. Continue making layers of tortillas, beans, scallions,

and cheese, ending with the bean mixture, until the dish is nearly full.

6. Bake in a moderate oven (350°F.) for 30 minutes, or until casserole is bubbling and heated through.

7. Sprinkle reserved cheese over casserole and return to oven just until cheese has melted. Remove from oven and top with remaining scallions.

8. Add any unused bean mixture to reserved sauce, heat and serve with the casserole. Pass a hot pepper sauce at the table. Serves 6.

I like to serve a large lettuce, tomato, cucumber, and avocado salad with an oil and lemon juice dressing with this casserole. A chilled egg custard makes a fitting dessert.

Beans combine with the versatile zucchini in this flavorful, cheese-topped casserole.

Layered Zucchini and Chili Beans

1 pound dried kidney beans
3 tablespoons olive oil
8 to 9 cups sliced zucchini
1 large onion, chopped
1 large green pepper, chopped
1 clove garlic, mashed
1 15-ounce can tomato sauce
2 tablespoons chili powder
¼ teaspoon ground cumin
a few sprigs fresh coriander, chopped
salt
8 ounces grated Monterey Jack cheese

1. Cook beans according to basic directions (see pages 23–26). Drain and reserve ¾ cup bean broth.

2. In a large, heavy skillet, heat 2 tablespoons of the oil and sauté zucchini slices. Remove zucchini from the skillet and set aside.

3. Put another tablespoon of oil in the skillet and sauté onion, pepper, and garlic until vegetables are tender.

4. Add tomato sauce, beans and reserved bean broth, chili powder, cumin, coriander, and salt. Bring to a boil, reduce heat, and simmer 10 minutes.

5. On the bottom of a deep 3-quart casserole dish, distribute evenly ⅓ of the zucchini. Remove 1 cup of sauce from the bean mixture and set aside. Pour ½ of the bean mixture over zucchini. Top with ⅓ of the cheese.

6. Make another layer using ⅓ of the zucchini, the remaining bean mixture, and another ⅓ of the cheese.

7. Add the remaining zucchini and top with reserved sauce.

8. Cover and bake in 350°F. oven about 25 minutes or until bubbling.

9. Sprinkle remaining cheese over top and place back into oven long enough to melt the cheese.

10. Remove from oven, garnish with a few coriander leaves, and serve immediately to 6.

I serve this with warm corn bread and a lettuce, tomato, avocado, and bean sprout salad with an oil and lemon juice dressing.

Everyone seems to like chili, and this is probably why there are so many chili recipes. This version, despite the lack of meat, has a rich flavor.

Chili

1 pound dried red kidney or pinto beans
2 onions, chopped
2 green peppers, coarsely chopped
1 small hot pepper, finely chopped
4 stalks celery, coarsely chopped
3 tablespoons peanut oil
½ teaspoon dried oregano
½ teaspoon ground cumin
2 tablespoons Mexican chili powder
1 28-ounce can plum tomatoes, chopped
1 teaspoon granulated fructose sugar
salt
a few sprigs of fresh coriander leaves, chopped (optional)

1. Cook beans according to basic directions (see pages 23–26).

2. Lightly brown onions, peppers, and celery in the oil. Add oregano, cumin, and chili powder. Cook the spices, while stirring, about 3 minutes.

3. Add tomatoes and cook until sauce is thick and vegetables are thoroughly cooked.

4. Add beans and bean broth, sugar, salt, and coriander. Bring to a boil, and when chili is piping hot serve to 6.

With chili I like corn bread and a tossed salad. My husband likes to top his bowl of chili with a little milk. Try it, it's good.

This untraditional chili, chock-full of vegetables, is nice and spicy and a favorite with my family.

Chili con Tofu

½ pound dried pinto beans
¼ cup peanut oil
1 large onion, chopped
1 clove garlic, mashed
1 large green pepper, coarsely chopped
1 or 2 small hot green peppers, seeded and finely chopped
2 stalks celery, coarsely chopped
2 large carrots, scraped and coarsely chopped
3 cups (about 1 pound) green beans, cut in ½ inch lengths (frozen
    green beans or fresh zucchini squash may be substituted)
2 cups sliced mushrooms
½ to 1 teaspoon cayenne
1 tablespoon paprika
1 teaspoon ground cumin
½ teaspoon oregano
1 28-ounce can thick tomato puree
1 cup water
1½ cups (about ½ pound) pressed bean curd (tofu) cut in small cubes
1 teaspoon lemon juice
salt
2 tablespoons chopped fresh coriander

1. Cook beans according to basic directions (see pages 23–26). Set aside.

2. Heat oil and sauté onion, garlic, green pepper, and

hot pepper, until onion is transparent. Add remaining vegetables and spices and continue to sauté about 5 more minutes.

3. Add tomato puree and water. Bring to a boil, reduce heat, and simmer until all vegetables are soft.

4. Shortly before serving add beans with their broth, tofu cubes, lemon juice, salt, and coriander. Bring to a boil, reduce heat, and simmer about 10 minutes to allow flavors to blend. Serves 6.

The chili goes well with whole wheat pita bread or over brown rice. A lettuce, tomato, and avocado salad with an oil and lemon juice dressing is a pleasant accompaniment.

This light, yet satisfying, casserole is always popular on a buffet table.

Chilies and Rice Casserole

½ pound dried pinto beans
2 cups brown rice
1 cup plain yoghurt
salt
1 7-ounce can whole green chilies, sliced
4 ounces sliced Monterey Jack cheese
3 eggs
2 cups milk
2 ounces grated sharp cheddar cheese

1. Cook beans according to basic directions (see pages 23–26). Drain.

2. Cook rice in double its volume of lightly salted water until water is absorbed and rice is tender.

3. Combine cooked rice, beans, yoghurt, and salt.

4. Spoon ⅓ of rice mixture into a deep, 3-quart, buttered casserole dish. Spread ½ of the sliced chilies evenly over rice mixture and put ½ of the Jack cheese over the chilies.

5. Beat eggs with milk and salt. Pour 1 cup of egg mixture over cheese in casserole dish.

6. Repeat layering of ingredients: ⅓ rice mixture, re-

maining chilies, remaining Jack cheese, and 1 cup of egg mixture.

7. Add remaining ⅓ of rice mixture, and then pour remaining egg mixture over top.

8. Poke a fork through in several places to allow egg and milk to seep through all layers.

9. Bake in a preheated oven at 350°F. for about 45 minutes. Sprinkle cheddar cheese on top and put back in oven until cheese is melted. Serves 6.

A colorful mixed vegetable salad goes nicely with this.

Frijoles, green onions, black olives, and cheddar cheese produce a tasty filling for these rolled corn tortillas which are topped with the delicious salsa rancheros.

Bean and Cheese Enchiladas

frijoles
salsa rancheros
oil for frying tortillas
1 dozen corn tortillas
green onions, chopped
pitted ripe olives, chopped
grated cheddar cheese
hot pepper sauce

1. Prepare frijoles according to recipe on page 157.
2. Prepare salsa rancheros according to recipe on page 158.
3. Heat a little oil in a skillet until very hot. Fry each tortilla just a few seconds on each side to soften. Drain tortillas on paper towels.
4. Along the center of each tortilla, place a heaping tablespoon of frijoles. Sprinkle with green onions and ripe olives. Place a heaping tablespoon of grated cheese on top.
5. Roll enchiladas and place in shallow baking dish with seam down. When all enchiladas are rolled and placed side by side in a baking dish, spoon salsa to cover enchiladas and bake in 350°F. oven about 20 minutes or until very hot.
6. Sprinkle grated cheese over enchiladas and return to oven until cheese melts. Serve with additional salsa and hot pepper sauce. Makes 12 enchiladas.

Frijoles can be used as a base for many Mexican dishes, including enchiladas, burritos, tostadas, tacos, nachos, and bean dip. They also can be eaten alone with warmed tortillas or Mexican rice.

If you eat Mexican food frequently, as we do, it is advisable to cook a large quantity of pinto beans. Freeze them in batches, and when you wish to have them, thaw and fry them up.

Frijoles

(Fried Beans)

½ pound dried pinto beans
2 tablespoons butter
1 tablespoon peanut oil
1 large onion, chopped
1 clove garlic, mashed
salt
1 cup grated Monterey Jack cheese

1. Cook beans according to basic directions (see pages 23–26). Drain, reserving about ¼ cup of bean broth.

2. Heat butter and peanut oil in a skillet. Cook onion and garlic until onion is thoroughly cooked but not browned.

3. Add drained beans and fry. Add the reserved bean broth and salt. Mash the beans as they fry, but not thoroughly.

4. Add cheese and stir until cheese is melted.

This tasty sauce is excellent over enchiladas and may be served with many Mexican dishes.

Salsa Rancheros

1 onion, chopped
1 clove garlic, mashed
2 fresh or canned jalapeño peppers, seeded and chopped
1 tablespoon butter
1 tablespoon peanut oil
1 3-ounce can green chilies, chopped
4 large fresh tomatoes, peeled and chopped (canned tomatoes may be substituted but fresh are preferred)
½ cup tomato juice or water
½ teaspoon liquid fructose sugar
2 tablespoons chopped fresh cilantro (coriander)
salt

1. Sauté onion, garlic, and jalapeño peppers, if fresh, in butter and oil until onion is well cooked but not browned.

2. Add chilies, and jalapeños if canned, tomatoes, tomato juice, fructose, cilantro, and salt. Cook slowly for 15 minutes.

Tacos are delicious and suitable for informal dining. Set out prepared tortillas, frijoles, cheese, sauce, and vegetables and let diners assemble their own tacos.

Tacos

12 corn tortillas
1 recipe frijoles, kept hot (see page 157)
½ pound (or more) grated cheddar cheese
hot pepper sauce or taco sauce
about 4 chopped green onions
about 4 chopped fresh tomatoes
½ head thinly sliced lettuce

1. Fry a tortilla in a little oil, over high heat, a few seconds on one side. Turn tortilla over and fold in half without creasing while frying the other side. Drain on paper towels while frying remaining tortillas.

2. Spread 1 or 2 heaping tablespoons of hot frijoles along the fold of the tortilla. Add some cheese, hot pepper sauce or taco sauce, green onions, tomatoes, and lettuce. Eat immediately! Serves 4 to 6.

Teenagers love these! Tostadas are tasty and easy to prepare, but do remember to provide large napkins with them because they are topped with lots of good things, they crunch, and occasionally spill over.

Tostadas

1 dozen corn tortillas
oil for frying
1 recipe frijoles (see page 157)
2 cups (or more) grated cheddar cheese
1 cup chopped green onions
½ head lettuce, shredded
2 avocados, sliced
3 or 4 large tomatoes, chopped
hot pepper sauce (optional)
sour cream (optional)

1. Fry tortillas on both sides in hot oil about ½ inch deep for 1 or 2 minutes or until crisp. Drain on absorbent paper.
2. Spread each tortilla with 1 heaping tablespoon of frijoles and sprinkle with a handful of cheese.
3. Broil tostadas just until cheese bubbles. (Broiling is not necessary, but I prefer them that way.)
4. On each tostada put some green onions, lettuce, avocado slices, tomatoes, and a few drops of hot pepper sauce.
5. Top with a dollop of sour cream, if desired. Serves 4 to 6.

Burritos can be made up in minutes once the frijoles are made and the vegetables are prepared. A blend of hot, cool, soft, crispy, and flavorful ingredients are wrapped in a tender flour tortilla.

Super Burritos

12 large flour tortillas
1 recipe frijoles, kept hot (see page 157)
½ cup chopped green onions
3 or 4 chopped fresh tomatoes
thinly sliced lettuce
2 avocados, sliced
hot pepper sauce

1. Heat each tortilla on a hot skillet a few seconds or until soft and pliable, or wrap the stack of tortillas in aluminum foil and warm in the oven.

2. Spread a large spoonful of hot frijoles down the center of the tortilla, leaving ½-inch margin at the top and 2 inches at the bottom.

3. Place on top of frijoles some green onions, tomatoes, lettuce, avocado slices, and a few drops of hot pepper sauce.

4. To wrap burrito, first fold up only the bottom 2 inches of the tortilla so as to cover part of the filling. Then fold sides toward center, overlapping each other to form a tight package. The top of the burrito is left open.

5. Fill all tortillas. Serve immediately.

The corn tortilla crumbs and the chilies add a unique flavor to these bean patties.

Pinto Patties with Spanish Rice

1 pound dried pinto beans
2 large onions, chopped
1 tablespoon peanut oil, plus peanut oil for frying
1 7-ounce can green chilies, chopped
5 or 6 corn tortillas
½ teaspoon oregano
¼ teaspoon ground cumin
salt
¼ teaspoon cayenne
1 egg, beaten
Monterey Jack cheese, sliced

1. Cook pinto beans according to basic directions (see pages 23–26). Drain and mash beans and put in large bowl.

2. Sauté onions in 1 tablespoon peanut oil until soft. Combine with chilies and remove from heat.

3. Add ½ the onion and chilies mixture to the mashed beans. Reserve the other ½ for the rice (see next recipe).

4. Break into pieces 2 of the tortillas and pulverize them in a blender. Add them to the beans, along with oregano, cumin, salt, and cayenne. Mix thoroughly and shape into 2½-inch patties.

5. Pulverize remaining tortillas and put them in a small bowl.

6. Dip patties in egg and then in tortilla crumbs. Fry in a little peanut oil until golden brown on one side. Turn, put a slice of cheese on top, and fry other side. Serve hot, plain or with salsa rancheros, and with Spanish rice.

A tossed salad of lettuce, tomatoes, and avocado with an oil and lemon juice dressing goes well with this meal.

Spanish Rice

½ onion-chilies mixture (see preceding recipe)
1½ cups brown rice
1 16-ounce can tomato sauce
1 cup water
salt

1. Sauté onion-chilies mixture with rice until rice turns opaque.

2. Add tomato sauce, water, and salt. Stir and bring to a boil over medium heat.

3. Reduce heat to low, put a tight-fitting lid on pan, and continue to cook for 25 to 45 minutes or until rice is thoroughly cooked and liquid is absorbed. Serves 6 to 8.

There are many versions of this popular and attractive rice dish from Central America. This particular one is from Santo Domingo.

Asopao

¾ cup dried red kidney beans
1 large onion, chopped
3 cloves garlic, mashed
4 tablespoons olive oil
1 green pepper, chopped
1 red pepper, chopped
1 or 2 hot green peppers, seeded and finely chopped
2 cups rice
6 cups vegetable broth (may be made from vegetable bouillon cubes)
2 rounded tablespoons tomato paste
1 tablespoon vinegar
¼ cup chopped fresh coriander leaves
¼ teaspoon oregano
salt
2 tablespoons capers
8 pimiento-stuffed green olives, sliced
1 cup fresh or frozen peas, lightly cooked and drained
¼ cup grated Parmesan cheese
2 or 3 hard-cooked eggs, sliced
4 canned pimientos, cut in strips

1. Cook kidney beans according to basic directions (see pages 23–26). Drain and keep warm.

2. In a large saucepan, sauté onion and garlic in 2 tablespoons of the olive oil until onion is transparent. Add peppers and continue to sauté until peppers are tender.

3. Add rice to pan and fry until grains of rice turn opaque. Stir so that the rice will not stick.

4. Add vegetable broth, tomato paste, vinegar, coriander, oregano, and salt. Bring to a boil, turn heat low, cover pan, and cook approximately 20 minutes. Rice should be soft. Add more broth if necessary to keep rice moist. Asopao means soupy.

5. Stir into rice, capers, olives, drained beans, peas, 2 tablespoons olive oil, and ½ of the Parmesan cheese. Adjust salt.

6. When asopao is piping hot, pour into a deep platter. Over the top, distribute evenly the remaining Parmesan cheese. Decorate with eggs and pimientos.

A large salad with fresh greens and tomato wedges with an olive oil and vinegar dressing is all that need follow this tasty dish.

This is a spicy dish with a delightful banana topping.

Caribbean Beans and Rice

1 pound dried red kidney beans
4 tablespoons butter
1 large onion, chopped
1 large green pepper, coarsely chopped
1 or 2 hot green peppers, finely chopped
3 cloves garlic, mashed
1 teaspoon curry powder
4 cups cooked brown rice
¼ cup chopped fresh coriander leaves
salt
2 firm bananas, sliced

1. Cook beans according to basic directions (see pages 23–26). Drain and reserve broth.

2. In a large heavy skillet, sauté in 2 tablespoons of the butter, onion, peppers, and garlic. When onions are transparent, add curry powder. Cook and stir until vegetables are lightly browned.

3. Add 1½ cups reserved bean broth and cook until vegetables are tender.

4. Add beans, rice, coriander, and salt. Cook until mixture is piping hot. Remove from heat, cover, and let stand a few minutes to allow flavors to blend.

5. Heat remaining 2 tablespoons butter in a small skillet. Add bananas and sauté until just heated through.

6. Pour beans and rice onto a serving platter. Spoon bananas and butter over top. Serves 6 to 8.

Accompany with a green or yellow vegetable and a salad. A cool custard would be a suitable dessert.

This nutritious dish, with its tantalizing flavors, takes little time to prepare.

Haitian Beans and Rice with Creole Sauce

¾ pound dried red kidney beans
¼ cup olive oil
1 large onion, chopped
2 large cloves garlic, mashed
4 whole cloves
1 2-inch stick cinnamon, broken in half
2 bay leaves
3 green peppers, coarsely chopped
1 hot chili pepper, finely chopped
¼ teaspoon oregano
¼ teaspoon ground cumin
salt
⅛ teaspoon white pepper
1½ cups brown rice

1. Cook beans according to basic directions (see pages 23–26). Drain and reserve broth.

2. In a large saucepan, sauté in olive oil, onion, garlic,

cloves, cinnamon stick, and bay leaves until onion is golden.

3. Add green peppers, chili pepper, oregano, cumin, salt, and white pepper. Continue to sauté until vegetables are lightly browned.

4. Stir in rice and cook over moderate heat until rice is opaque. Add 3½ cups combined reserved bean broth and water, stir, and bring to a boil. Reduce heat and simmer, covered, for 20 minutes.

5. Combine rice mixture and beans and transfer to a covered, 3-quart baking dish.

6. Bake in a preheated 350°F. oven for 25 minutes or until liquid is absorbed and rice is thoroughly cooked.

7. Remove from oven, let stand for 10 minutes, uncover and fluff with a fork. Serves 6. Pass creole sauce at the table.

Creole Sauce

1 cup peeled and chopped tomatoes (fresh preferred)
1 tablespoon thick tomato puree
juice from 1 juicy lime
1 green onion, finely chopped
1 tablespoon finely chopped celery
1 small hot pepper, finely minced
¼ teaspoon liquid fructose sugar
salt
dash white pepper

1. Combine all ingredients in a small bowl. Stir until thoroughly blended.

2. Serve with Haitian Beans and Rice.

An unusual combination—the recipe comes from Colombia.

Lolita's Red Beans

1 pound dried red kidney beans
1 onion, chopped
2 tablespoons butter
1 small (6 or 7 cups) cabbage, coarsely chopped
½ cup chili sauce or catsup
salt
dash white pepper

1. Cook beans according to basic directions (see pages 23–26). Drain and reserve broth.
2. In a large saucepan, sauté onion in butter until it is soft and lightly browned.
3. Add cabbage and about 1 cup of reserved bean broth and cook until cabbage is tender.
4. Shortly before serving, add beans with remaining broth, chili sauce, salt, and pepper.
5. Mix thoroughly, bring to a boil, reduce heat, and simmer 5 minutes. Serve immediately to 6 or 8.

I like to serve corn bread and a tossed salad with this. A fruit compote makes a pleasing dessert.

This Cuban national dish of black beans is served with white rice—hence the name, "Moors and Christians."

Moros y Cristianos

1 pound dried black beans
1 large onion, chopped
2 cloves garlic, mashed
1 large green pepper, chopped
2 cups chopped celery
½ teaspoon dried marjoram
½ teaspoon ground cumin
3 tablespoons olive oil
salt
hot pepper sauce

166

1. Cook beans according to basic directions (see pages 23–26). Drain, reserving broth.

2. Sauté onion, garlic, green pepper, celery, marjoram, and cumin in olive oil until vegetables are lightly browned. Add 1½ cups reserved bean broth. Cover pan and cook until vegetables are tender.

3. Combine vegetable mixture with beans. Add salt and hot pepper sauce. Bring to a boil, reduce heat, and simmer 10 minutes to allow flavors to blend. Serves 6 to 8.

Serve with rice, a cooked green or yellow vegetable, and a salad.

India
&
Pakistan

India and Pakistan

My dear friend Hansa Pandya prepares a superb dal in the style of her family of the Gujarat state in India. Her family is strictly vegetarian, as are most Indians in this area, the home of Mahatma Gandhi. They have some sort of dal and vegetables, yoghurt, and grains daily. Hansa, who has taught me much about Indian cooking, has lived in Western countries for many years and combines her Indian diet with vegetarian foods from the West.

Hansa's Dal

1 pound tur or toor dal
3 tablespoons peanut oil
1 teaspoon black mustard seeds
½ teaspoon whole cumin seeds
1 teaspoon fenugreek (methi)
¼ teaspoon asafetida (hing)
8 to 10 curry leaves (neem)
1½ tablespoons ground coriander
1 tablespoon ground cumin
1 teaspoon garamasala
1 teaspoon turmeric
½ teaspoon cayenne (or to taste)
½ of a 6-ounce can of tomato paste
1½ tablespoons natural sugar (jaggery, the natural sugar of India, is best)
juice of 1 lemon
salt
1½ tablespoons finely minced fresh ginger

1. Cook dal according to basic directions (see pages 23–26), using 9 cups of water, until very soft and disintegrating.

2. In a small saucepan, heat peanut oil. When it is very hot, add mustard seeds. When they begin to pop, add cumin seeds, fenugreek, asafetida, and curry leaves. Remove pan from heat, swirl, and pour hot oil and seeds into cooked dal. It will sputter, so stand back.

3. Add ground coriander, ground cumin, garamasala, turmeric, cayenne, tomato paste, and sugar. Simmer, uncovered, stirring occasionally, about 15 minutes to allow flavors to blend and mixture to thicken slightly.

4. Add lemon juice, salt, and ginger. Simmer an additional 5 minutes. Adjust seasonings. This dal should be quite thin and soupy. Serves 6 or more.

A tasty addition is spicy noodles (dal dhokari) cooked in the dal (recipe follows).

Serve in small bowls along with rice, spiced vegetables, salad, yoghurt, and Indian pickles, if desired.

Ingredients can be found in special foods stores where Indian foods are sold or can be ordered by mail.

Dal Dhokari is a savory dough made of whole wheat and chick-pea flours, rolled out in very thin strips like noodles, and cooked in a thin dal such as Hansa's.

The strips also can be fried in hot oil or the dough can be rolled out in about 4- or 5-inch circles and fried like chapatis or tortillas on a dry skillet. These produce a spicy and delicious snack.

Dal Dhokari

1½ cups whole wheat flour
¼ cup chick-pea flour (besan)
¼ teaspoon ajway or ajawan seeds
¼ teaspoon whole cumin seeds
½ teaspoon ground cumin
¼ teaspoon asafetida
¼ teaspoon turmeric
1 teaspoon ground coriander
salt
¼ teaspoon cayenne
2¼ tablespoons peanut oil
¾ cup warm water

1. Combine dry ingredients in a bowl.

2. Add oil and mix well.

3. Add warm water, gradually, until the dough is soft and pliable and can be rolled out easily.

4. Cover dough and let stand for an hour or longer.

5. Roll out dough very thinly as you would to make noodles and cut in 1 × 2-inch strips. Drop into boiling dal, after dal is cooked, and boil until done.

6. For snacks, fry the dough strips in ½ inch of hot oil until crisp, or shape the dough into small balls, each about the size of a large walnut. Flatten and roll out each ball with a rolling pin until it is round and flat like a small tortilla or chapati.

7. Heat an ungreased, heavy skillet until a drop of water flicked on it sizzles instantly. Fry dhokari rounds on both sides until cooked. Some dark spots will appear.

This recipe was given to me in 1973 by V. G. Dave, a Gujarati Indian in Kenya who owned and operated the Supreme Hotel and vegetarian restaurant in Nairobi. I will never forget the many delicious meals we had there.

For about $1, a diner would receive a large stainless steel plate (thali) with little stainless bowls (katoris) set around the edge of the thali to hold the spicy, aromatic, cooked vegetables. In the center would be hot, tender, freshly made chapatis (the flat, round, unleavened, Indian, whole wheat bread), rice, and a larger katori to hold the delicious, traditional Gujarati dal. Waiters constantly went around the tables refilling empty bowls and bringing hot, buttered (with ghee) chapatis as quickly as they were made.

On the tables were trays of freshly cut vegetables with lots of chilies and quartered limes, and each person was served a tall glass of lassi, a cold yoghurt drink.

Dave also had for sale a great assortment of freshly made Indian sweets and savory snacks that were just as delicious and attractive as the meal. I never could walk by that display without having my resistance give way to temptation.

Tur Dal

1 pound oily tur dal
3 tablespoons peanut oil
1 teaspoon black mustard seeds
1 teaspoon fenugreek
⅛ teaspoon asafetida
¼ teaspoon cayenne
1 teaspoon turmeric
1 teaspoon ground coriander
1 teaspoon ground cumin
6 curry leaves (optional)
1 cup tomatoes, peeled and chopped (fresh is better)
1 tablespoon Indian raw sugar *(jaggery)* or fructose sugar
3 tablespoons lemon juice
1 fresh hot chili pepper, quartered
2 tablespoons chopped fresh coriander leaves
salt

1. Wash dal in warm water, rubbing it between your hands, and cook according to basic directions (see pages

23–26), using 7 cups water, until dal has almost dissolved. Stir occasionally.

2. In a small saucepan, heat peanut oil until very hot. Add black mustard seeds, and when they begin to pop, add fenugreek, asafetida, and cayenne. Remove from heat when fenugreek turns a shade darker but before it burns, and pour the spices and oil into the pan of cooked dal. Be careful when doing this because the oil will sputter when it hits the dal.

3. Add to the dal, turmeric, ground coriander, cumin, curry leaves, tomatoes, sugar, lemon juice, and chili pepper. Cook 15 minutes.

4. Add coriander leaves and salt. Add a little water if dal is too thick. This dal should be thin, like soup. Cook another 3 minutes and serve in small bowls to 6 or more.

The whole mung or moong beans, as used in this recipe, are a deep green. Some dal preparations are made with split mung beans or whole mung which have had the skins removed, in which case the color is pale yellow.

Spicy Mung Bean Dal

1 cup whole mung beans
2 onions, sliced
1 clove garlic, mashed
2 tablespoons peanut oil
½ teaspoon ground ginger
1 teaspoon garamasala
1 teaspoon turmeric
1 tablespoon ground coriander
¼ teaspoon cayenne
1 cup chopped tomatoes, fresh or canned
a few sprigs fresh coriander, chopped
juice of ½ lemon (2 tablespoons)
3 tablespoons plain yoghurt

1. Cook mung beans according to basic directions (see pages 23–26) using 4 cups water.

2. Sauté onions and garlic in peanut oil until onions

turn golden. Add ginger, garamasala, turmeric, ground coriander, and cayenne. Continute to sauté about 10 minutes, while stirring so that spices do not stick.

3. Add tomatoes and fresh coriander and cook another 10 minutes, stirring occasionally. Remove from heat and add lemon juice.

4. Put mung beans with broth and spice mixture through the blender, in batches, and pour puree into a saucepan.

5. Stir in yoghurt and simmer 10 minutes. Serves 4.

Serve over steamed brown rice and with a cooked vegetable such as peas and carrots. Add a salad and some yoghurt.

Dal and vegetables combine very well. The vegetables provide not only added vitamins but flavor and color as well.

Dal with Zucchini

½ pound split and peeled mung or moong dal
1 medium-large (2 pounds) zucchini squash
1 tablespoon peeled and finely chopped fresh ginger
1 or 2 hot green chili peppers, quartered
3 cloves garlic, mashed
1 tablespoon ground coriander
1 teaspoon ground cumin
2 teaspoons natural sugar (Indian jaggery is best)
¼ teaspoon turmeric
2½ tablespoons peanut oil
½ teaspoon black mustard seeds
1 dried red chili pepper
½ teaspoon whole cumin seeds
½ teaspoon fenugreek
⅛ teaspoon asafetida
salt
1 tablespoon chopped fresh coriander
1 tablespoon lemon juice

1. Cook dal according to basic directions (see pages 23–26).

2. Quarter zucchini lengthwise and slice. Cook in minimum amount of water until tender.

3. Combine dal, zucchini (with its cooking water), gin-

ger, chilies, garlic, ground coriander, ground cumin, sugar, and turmeric. Simmer 5 minutes.

4. Heat oil in a small saucepan. When hot, add black mustard seeds. When they begin to pop, add dried chili pepper, cumin seeds, fenugreek, and asafetida. When the spices turn a shade darker, but before they burn, pour hot oil and spices into dal. Simmer dal 10 minutes.

5. Add salt, fresh coriander, and lemon juice. Cook 2 minutes and serve to 4.

Chapatis and/or rice as well as cool, plain yoghurt always go well with dal. It can be accompanied by a tossed salad and Indian pickles.

This is very easy to prepare and has a wonderful flavor.

Indian Split Peas with Green Beans

½ pound yellow split peas
2 tablespoons peanut oil
1 onion, chopped
1 1-inch cube fresh ginger, peeled and minced
1 small hot chili pepper, chopped
½ teaspoon turmeric
1 pound green beans, cut in 1-inch lengths
½ cup water
salt
1 tablespoon chopped fresh coriander
1 tablespoon lemon juice (or to taste)

1. Cook split peas according to basic directions (see pages 23–26).

2. Heat peanut oil in saucepan and sauté onion, ginger, and chili pepper. (You can remove seeds from chili if you think it will be too hot.)

3. When onion is lightly browned, add turmeric. Cook and stir a few seconds and add green beans and water. Cover pan and simmer until beans are tender.

4. Shortly before serving, add the split peas, salt, co-

riander, and lemon juice. When completely heated through, serve with brown rice or chapatis. Serves 4.

I always serve yoghurt with this for its cooling effect. Sliced tomatoes, cucumbers, and avocados are a compatible addition.

This is one of my family's favorite meals. The sambar can be eaten with rice. However, the combination of sambar and pancakes with yoghurt and condiments makes an enticing and nutritious eating experience.

South Indian Sambar with Savory Pancakes

(Spicy Lentils with Savory Pancakes)

½ cup red lentils
½ cup tur dal ⎫ as an alternative, use 1½ cups
½ cup yellow split peas ⎭ yellow split peas
3 carrots, sliced
2 potatoes, cubed
1 onion, chopped
2 cups eggplant cubes or other vegetable of your choice, such as green beans, cauliflower, or broccoli
1 tablespoon garamasala
1 teaspoon turmeric
1 tablespoon sambar powder or curry powder
2 tablespoons peanut oil
½ teaspoon black mustard seeds
1 cinnamon stick, broken in half
3 whole cloves
½ teaspoon fenugreek seeds
juice of 1 lemon
salt

1. Cook lentils together according to basic directions (see pages 23–26) using 5 cups water.

2. Vegetables may be cooked with the lentils after the lentils have soaked, but for better digestibility, I prefer cooking vegetables separately in 1 cup water. Cook vegetables until tender but not falling apart.

3. When lentils are soft, add garamasala, turmeric, sam-

176

bar or curry powder, and vegetables, with any remaining water if cooked separately.

4. Heat peanut oil in a small saucepan. When hot, add black mustard seeds, cinnamon stick, and cloves. When seeds begin to pop, add fenugreek. Swirl seeds around in the oil, and when fenugreek seeds turn a shade darker (be careful not to burn them), pour oil and spices into lentils.

5. Add lemon juice and salt. Cook together about 10 minutes and serve over savory pancakes. Serves 6.

I like this with plain yoghurt and condiments such as lime pickle and sweet mango chutney. Put them all on the plate at once.

These go well with sambar and they also make tasty snacks on their own.

Savory Pancakes

1 cup semolina (fine grained)
½ cup chick-pea flour (also called besan and gram flour)
1 or 2 hot green peppers, seeded and finely chopped
1 rounded tablespoon finely chopped or grated fresh ginger
1 teaspoon salt
2 tablespoons peanut oil
¾ cup plain yoghurt
¾ cup water

1. Mix semolina and chick-pea flour.
2. Combine with pepper, ginger, salt, oil, and yoghurt.
3. Gradually add water and stir until batter is smooth. Let sit 1 hour before making pancakes. Batter will thicken. Add water if necessary.
4. Pour large spoonfuls of batter on a hot, lightly oiled, griddle, spreading batter to make 4-inch pancakes about ¼ inch thick.
5. Cook pancakes until lightly browned on bottom, about 3 minutes. Turn pancakes and cook other side about 2 or 3 minutes.
6. Continue cooking pancakes until all batter is used. Makes 12. Serve with sambar.

Channa dal takes longer to cook than other Indian dals, about 1 to 1½ hours, but it has an exceptionally pleasant flavor.

Split Channa Dal of Bihar

½ pound split channa dal
2 tablespoons peanut oil
½ teaspoon whole cumin seeds
½ teaspoon fenugreek
1 large onion, chopped
4 cloves garlic, mashed
2 fresh hot peppers, seeded and finely chopped
1 teaspoon turmeric
¼ teaspoon cayenne
several sprigs fresh coriander, chopped
salt

1. Cook dal in 4 cups water according to basic directions (see pages 23–26).

2. In a skillet, heat peanut oil and add cumin seeds and fenugreek. When they turn a shade darker, add onion, garlic, and hot peppers. Sauté until onion is transparent.

3. Add turmeric and cayenne and continue to sauté, while stirring, for 2 or 3 minutes.

4. Add about ½ cup of broth from the pan of cooked dal and simmer until onion is soft.

5. Shortly before serving, add onion mixture to the dal. When dal is very hot, add coriander and salt. Cook an additional 2 or 3 minutes and serve to 3 or 4.

Serve with basmati rice or chapatis, cooked spinach or other green vegetable, yoghurt, and Indian pickles.

There are many versions of this basic dish of Indian dal cooked with rice. This khitcheri is yellow because the mung or moong dal is split and the outer green coating has been removed. It is very tasty and simple to prepare.

Khitcheri

(Lentils and Rice)

1 cup brown rice
½ cup split mung or moong dal
2 tablespoons peanut oil
1 onion, chopped
1 clove garlic, finely minced
1 rounded tablespoon finely minced fresh ginger
1 small hot chili pepper, finely minced
1 teaspoon turmeric
½ teaspoon ground cumin
1 teaspoon garamasala
salt
butter

1. Soak rice in sufficient water to cover by ½ inch.
2. Rinse dal and put in saucepan with water to cover by 1 inch. Bring to a rolling boil and allow to boil 1 minute. Cover pan, remove from heat, and allow to soak for 2 hours.
3. In a large saucepan, heat peanut oil and fry onion, garlic, ginger, and chili pepper until onion is soft.
4. Add drained rice and drained dal to the pan. (Reserve soaking water from rice and dal.) Add turmeric, cumin, and garamasala, and fry, while stirring, over medium heat for about 5 minutes.
5. Add 2½ cups of the reserved soaking water, using first that from the dal and adding some from the rice. Add salt. Bring to a boil, lower heat, cover pan, and simmer until liquid is absorbed and rice and dal are cooked. Add water as necessary. Khitcheri is not supposed to be too dry.
6. Serve on plates with a lump of butter on each portion. Serves 4.

A curried vegetable and yoghurt go nicely with khitcheri.

179

My Indian friends tell me that urad dal has the highest protein content of any of the dals. Mrs. Pushkar Oza of Bombay, India, reputedly a fine cook, shared her recipes for black and white urad dals and for whole urad. Black and white urad is the same dal. Black has the skin on it and the white has had the skin removed. Urad dal is not readily available, but stores carrying foods of India should have it.

Split Black Urad Dal

1 cup black urad dal, split
1 1-inch cube fresh ginger, finely chopped
1 clove garlic, mashed
1 hot chili pepper, quartered
½ teaspoon turmeric
2 tablespoons peanut oil
½ teaspoon fenugreek
⅛ teaspoon asafetida
¼ teaspoon cayenne
1 cup buttermilk

1. Cook dal according to basic directions (see pages 23–26) until dal is soft. It will absorb much of the water. Add the ginger, garlic, chili, and turmeric and continue to cook while you fry the spices.

2. In a small saucepan heat peanut oil. When very hot, add fenugreek, asafetida, and cayenne. Remove pan from heat so that fenugreek does not burn. It should, however, darken. Pour the hot spices and oil into the dal. Be careful, as it will sputter a little. Add buttermilk and cook about 5 minutes. Serves 3 or 4.

Urad dal usually is eaten with chapatis, but it may be eaten with brown rice as well. Indians often put ghee (clarified butter) on the dal and have a little jaggery on the thali. They also have a special eggplant preparation with urad dal. This is considered a meal to be eaten in winter.

White Urad Dal

1½ cups white urad dal, split
3 tablespoons peanut oil
½ teaspoon black mustard seeds
½ teaspoon whole cumin seeds
½ teaspoon fenugreek
⅛ teaspoon asafetida
⅛ to ¼ teaspoon cayenne
½ teaspoon ground cumin
1 teaspoon turmeric
½ cup chopped tomatoes
1 fresh hot chili pepper, quartered
salt
2 tablespoons lemon juice
1 tablespoon chopped fresh coriander

1. Cook dal according to basic directions (see pages 23–26). Do not allow it to disintegrate, but cook until soft.

2. In a small saucepan, heat peanut oil until very hot. Add black mustard seeds. When they begin to pop, add cumin seeds, fenugreek, asafetida, and cayenne. Remove pan from heat so that the spices do not burn and immediately add hot spices and oil to cooked dal. Be careful when doing this because it will splatter.

3. Add to the dal, ground cumin, turmeric, tomatoes, and chili pepper. Cook about 15 minutes. Shortly before serving, add salt, lemon juice, and coriander. Serves 6.

This is usually eaten with chapatis and/or rice and an eggplant dish.

Whole urad dal with the skins on takes about 1½ to 2 hours to cook. It is not a smooth mixture as are most dals, but it is tasty and extremely nutritious. It is usually eaten in the winter months in India because it is thought to give one the added energy needed to combat the cold.

Whole Black Urad Dal

½ pound whole black urad dal
2 tablespoons peanut oil
1 teaspoon sesame seeds
½ teaspoon fenugreek
⅛ teaspoon asafetida
1 large clove garlic, mashed
½ cup unsweetened dried or fresh grated coconut
1 tablespoon finely chopped fresh ginger
1 or 2 hot green chili peppers, chopped
½ teaspoon turmeric
¼ teaspoon ajawan seeds
¼ teaspoon cayenne
½ cup yoghurt
2 tablespoons chick-pea flour (besan or gram flour)
salt
a few sprigs fresh coriander, chopped
2 tablespoons butter

1. Cook dal according to basic directions (pages 23–26).

2. In a large saucepan, heat peanut oil. When hot, add sesame seeds, fenugreek and asafetida. Swirl around in the pan, and when the fenugreek darkens a little, remove from heat.

3. Add 1 cup broth from cooked dal, garlic, coconut, ginger, chilies, turmeric, ajawan seeds, and cayenne. Cook 15 minutes.

4. Combine yoghurt, chick-pea flour, and ¼ cup dal broth. Stir vigorously to remove lumps.

5. Add dal, yoghurt mixture, and salt to saucepan. Cook 10 minutes. Add coriander and cook another 2 minutes.

6. Just before serving, stir in butter. Serves 4.

Chapatis go well with this, as does brown rice. It is usually eaten with an eggplant dish and yoghurt.

Mrs. Oza also highly recommends this eggplant dish, especially to accompany urad dal.

Mrs. Oza's Spiced Eggplant

1 medium to large eggplant
2 tablespoons peanut oil
pinch of asafetida
1 small (¼ cup) onion, chopped
⅛ teaspoon cayenne
1 teaspoon ground coriander
½ teaspoon turmeric
salt
¼ cup yoghurt
a few sprigs fresh coriander, chopped

1. Pierce the eggplant in a few places, then put in a baking dish and bake in 400°F. oven for about 45 minutes or until soft. If eggplant begins scorching, reduce heat.

2. When eggplant is cool enough to handle, peel and cut in 1-inch cubes.

3. Heat peanut oil in a skillet and add asafetida. After 3 or 4 seconds add onion and stir.

4. Stir in cayenne, ground coriander, and turmeric. Cook, while stirring, until onion is well done but not browned.

5. Add eggplant and salt and turn the eggplant pieces with a spoon or spatula until they are coated with the onion mixture.

6. Reduce heat to low, cover skillet, and cook, stirring occasionally, until eggplant is thoroughly cooked.

7. Stir in yoghurt and fresh coriander and simmer 5 minutes longer. Serves 3 or 4.

Serve with urad dal or with any South Asian dish.

Val, India's white beans, are prepared by Hansa Pandya in the style of the Gujarat. Gujarati dishes usually are sweetened with jaggery and have a souring agent such as tamarind or lemon juice in them to give them a distinctive, slightly sweet and sour flavor.

Hansa's Val

(Indian White Beans)

1 pound val (great northern beans may be substituted)
5 tablespoons peanut oil
1¼ teaspoons ajawan seeds
1½ teaspoons black mustard seeds
½ teaspoon fenugreek
¼ teaspoon asafetida
salt
1 teaspoon turmeric
½ teaspoon ground cumin
1 teaspoon ground coriander
½ teaspoon cayenne
1 teaspoon garamasala
1 tablespoon tamarind extract (lemon juice, to taste, may be
  substituted)
4 cloves garlic, mashed
1½ tablespoons jaggery or other natural sugar
2 tablespoons chick-pea flour (besan or gram), diluted in a little water

1. Cook beans according to basic directions (see pages 23–26).

2. In a large saucepan, heat peanut oil. When hot, add the ajawan seeds, black mustard seeds, fenugreek, and asafetida. When the seeds pop, add cooked beans and their broth. Be careful not to burn spices.

3. Add remaining ingredients and cook for 20 minutes or until thickened and flavors have blended. Serves 6.

Chapatis go exceptionally well with val, as does yoghurt. You can follow this with a salad and a cooked vegetable.

184

My friend Lakshmi Crane, who is from Trinidad, of East Indian origin, and now resides in Syracuse, New York, provides this recipe of her mother's. Lakshmi cooks both South Asian and Caribbean foods. In this recipe, she has prepared lima beans, native of South America, in the style of Benares and the Bihar province of India.

Lakshmi's Indian Lima Beans

1 pound dried lima beans
2 tablespoons ground coriander
2 teaspoons ground cumin
1 teaspoon black mustard seeds
4 tablespoons peanut oil
2 large onions, chopped
6 cloves garlic, mashed
2 tablespoons fresh ginger, peeled and finely chopped
2 or 3 fresh hot peppers, seeded and chopped
2 cups peeled and chopped tomatoes
2 tablespoons lemon juice
a few sprigs of fresh coriander, chopped
salt

1. Cook beans according to basic directions (see pages 23–26). Drain, reserving 1 cup bean broth.

2. Sauté ground coriander, ground cumin, and mustard seeds in peanut oil, about 1 minute, over medium high heat. Add onions, garlic, ginger, and hot peppers. Cook and stir until onion is lightly browned.

3. Add tomatoes and continue cooking until most of the liquid has been absorbed and mixture has cooked down to a paste, about 20 minutes. Stir occasionally, while cooking, so it will not stick.

4. Combine tomato mixture with limas and reserved broth, lemon juice, fresh coriander, and salt. Cook until piping hot. Serve immediately to 6 or 8.

This goes well with rice or chapatis, cool yoghurt, and a salad.

Lakshmi's Lentils

1 pound lentils
3 tablespoons peanut oil
1 teaspoon ground cumin
1 teaspoon fenugreek
3 medium onions, chopped
3 cloves garlic, mashed
1 or 2 hot green chili peppers, cut in pieces
1 bay leaf
1 clove
pinch ground cardamom
¾ cup cream
salt

1. Cook lentils according to basic directions (see pages 23–26). If you would like the lentils soupy, leave the broth. If you prefer them thick, drain the broth, or some of it, according to your taste.

2. Heat peanut oil in a skillet. When hot, add cumin and fenugreek. When they begin to darken, add onions, garlic, chilies, bay leaf, and clove. Lower heat and sauté until onions are soft and lightly browned.

3. Turn up heat again, and when contents of skillet are very hot, pour into lentils.

4. Add cardamom and cook for 10 minutes.

5. Add cream and salt, and when lentils are very hot, but not boiling, serve over brown rice. Serves 6 to 8.

Serve with a cooked green or yellow vegetable.

Beans with spices make for exciting cuisine. Rajma is a good example.

Rajma

(Curried Red Kidney Beans)

½ pound dried red kidney beans
¼ cup peanut oil
1 onion, chopped
1 hot green chili pepper, chopped
1 tablespoon finely chopped fresh ginger
1 large (or 2 small) cloves garlic, mashed
1 2-inch stick cinnamon, broken in half
2 whole cloves
2 whole cardamom pods
1 tablespoon ground coriander
1 teaspoon turmeric
½ teaspoon ground cumin
½ cup peeled and diced ripe tomatoes
a few sprigs fresh coriander leaves, chopped
¼ cup plain yoghurt
salt

1. Cook beans according to basic directions (see pages 23–26).

2. In a large saucepan, heat peanut oil over medium heat and fry onion, pepper, ginger, garlic, cinnamon stick, cloves, and cardamom pods until onion is soft and just beginning to brown.

3. Add ground coriander, turmeric, and cumin and continue to cook and stir for 5 minutes. Add tomato and cook and stir until mixture loses most of its moisture and becomes a paste.

4. Pour beans and bean broth over the paste and stir. Bring to a boil, lower heat, and let simmer for a few minutes to allow flavors to blend.

5. Shortly before serving, add fresh coriander leaves. Mix yoghurt with a tablespoon of the gravy and whisk it thoroughly before adding it to the curry. Add salt. Serves 3 or 4.

This goes well over rice. Serve lots of yoghurt and a salad.

A classic recipe and an easy preparation, this comes from an Indian student's home in New Delhi, India.

Asha's Channa Curry

(Chick-Pea Curry)

1 pound dried chick-peas
1 large onion, chopped
2 tablespoons finely chopped fresh ginger
1 or 2 fresh hot chili peppers, finely chopped
2 sticks cinnamon, broken in half
4 whole cloves
6 cardamom pods
3 tablespoons butter or peanut oil
1 tablespoon ground coriander
1 teaspoon ground cumin
1 teasoon curry powder
¼ teaspoon ground ginger
1 6-ounce can tomato paste
3 rounded tablespoons plain yoghurt
salt
several sprigs fresh coriander, chopped

1. Cook chick-peas according to basic directions (see pages 23–26). Drain, reserving broth.

2. In a large saucepan, sauté onion, fresh ginger, chili pepper, cinnamon sticks, cloves, and cardamom pods in the butter until onion is cooked but not brown.

3. Add ground coriander, cumin, curry powder, and ground ginger and continue to sauté and stir for 5 or 6 minutes. Stir in tomato paste and ½ cup reserved chick-pea broth. Cook and stir another 5 minutes.

4. Add chick-peas and enough additional broth to make a thick sauce, and bring mixture to a slow boil.

5. Combine yoghurt with a little of the sauce and add it to the curry. Add salt and fresh coriander and simmer about 5 minutes. Serves 6 to 8.

Serve with chapatis or with brown rice. I also like to serve with this curry, a bowl of cool yoghurt, a plate of thinly sliced raw vegetables, such as tomatoes, green peppers, cucumbers, green onions, carrots, and avocados, with a squeeze of lime juice over them, a sweet chutney, and a lime or mango pickle. The chutney and pickle can be purchased in specialty food stores.

Aloo Chole is a spicy dish from the Punjab state in northern India. The people of the Punjab are mostly agriculturists and are tall and strong. The Sikh men of the Punjab never cut their hair, wear turbans, and are considered to be excellent soldiers.

Aloo Chole

(Potatoes and Chick-Peas)

1 pound dried chick-peas
⅓ cup peanut oil
1 or 2 dried chili peppers, broken in pieces
6 bay leaves
1½ teaspoons whole cumin seeds
1 teaspoon black mustard seeds
¼ teaspoon asafetida
1 large onion, chopped
1½ pounds potatoes, unpeeled, cut in 1-inch pieces
2 teaspoons garamasala
1½ teaspoons turmeric
2 teaspoons ground coriander
1 teaspoon ground cumin
salt
¼ to ½ teaspoon cayenne
1 tablespoon jaggery (or any natural sugar)
2 cloves garlic, mashed
1 tablespoon tamarind extract (lemon juice to taste may be substituted)
3 tablespoons tomato puree

1. Cook chick-peas according to basic directions (see pages 23–26). Drain and reserve broth.
2. Heat peanut oil in a 3-quart saucepan and fry chili peppers, bay leaves, cumin seeds, black mustard seeds, and asafetida. When seeds begin to pop, add onion and potatoes and continue to fry. When onion and potatoes are lightly browned, add reserved chick-pea broth and cook with a lid on the pan until vegetables are tender.
3. Add remaining ingredients, including chick-peas. Bring to a boil, reduce heat, and simmer 10 minutes to allow flavors to blend. Serves 6 to 8.

Serve with chapatis or brown rice, yoghurt, and a salad.

189

Eggplant and chick-peas go particularly well together. This is an exceptionally delicious blending of the two, and is easy to prepare.

Eggplant and Chick-Peas

½ pound dried chick-peas
¼ cup peanut oil
1 large onion, chopped
¼ teaspoon whole cumin seeds
1 hot green chili pepper, chopped
1 large eggplant, cut in 1-inch cubes
salt
½ teaspoon turmeric
1 teaspoon ground coriander
1 tablespoon chopped fresh coriander (optional)
1 tablespoon lemon juice (or to taste)

1. Cook chick-peas according to basic directions (see pages 23–26). Drain.

2. Heat peanut oil in large, heavy skillet, and sauté onion until transparent. Add cumin seeds and chili pepper and sauté and stir for 2 minutes.

3. Add eggplant to the skillet, along with salt, turmeric, and ground coriander. Continue to fry and stir about 5 minutes longer. Cover skillet, reduce heat, and cook another 5 minutes or until eggplant is done.

4. Shortly before serving, add drained chick-peas, fresh coriander, and lemon juice. Bring to a boil, reduce heat, and simmer a few minutes to blend flavors. Adjust salt and lemon juice. Serves 4.

This goes well with chapatis and rice and, of course, yoghurt.

*Pilau, a sumptuous and attractive Muslim dish, is usually
served at special occasions. It was cherished by the Great Moguls
who ruled over India for three centuries.*

Kashmiri Pilau

½ pound dried chick-peas
2 tablespoons peanut oil
3 tablespoons butter
2 onions, chopped
4 cloves garlic, mashed
1 1-inch cube ginger, finely minced
¼ teaspoon cayenne
4 whole cloves
6 cardamom pods
1 2-inch stick of cinnamon, broken in half
1 cup diced carrots
1 cup sliced mushrooms
1 cup green beans, cut in ½-inch lengths
2 tomatoes, peeled and chopped
½ teaspoon turmeric
2 cups long-grain rice (Indian Basmati rice is best—rinse before
  cooking)
1 cup frozen green peas
½ to 1 teaspoon saffron
1 teaspoon chopped fresh mint leaves or ½ teaspoon dried
½ cup raisins
2 vegetable bouillon cubes
salt
½ cup raw cashews, halves and pieces

1. Cook chick-peas according to basic directions (see
pages 23–26). Drain, reserving broth.

2. In a large saucepan, heat peanut oil and 2 tablespoons of the butter and sauté onions, garlic, ginger, cayenne, cloves, cardamon pods, and cinnamon stick. Cook
until onions are soft and golden, but not browned.

3. Add carrots, mushrooms, and green beans and continue to sauté for 5 minutes.

4. Add tomatoes and sauté another 3 minutes.

5. Add 1 cup of reserved chick-pea broth and turmeric.
Cover pan and cook until vegetables are nearly done.

6. Butter a large, shallow baking dish and add rice,

peas, chick-peas, vegetable mixture, saffron, mint leaves, and raisins.

7. Dissolve vegetable bouillon cubes in 3¾ cups hot bean broth and water mixture and add to baking dish. Add salt and mix well.

8. Cover and bake in 350°F. oven 1 hour or until rice is tender and liquid is absorbed.

9. Sauté cashews in remaining 1 tablespoon butter, while stirring, until cashews are very lightly browned. Spoon cashews evenly over pilau and serve to 6 or 8.

Precede the pilau with a creamed soup. Then, with the pilau, serve a salad of romaine lettuce, tomato wedges, red onion rings, and cucumber slices with an oil and lemon juice dressing. Top off the meal with mango slices and lychees for a rewarding and exotic dining experience.

Our friend Noorali Velji is an Ismaili from Tanzania now practicing law in Washington, D.C. When his wife, Shirin, goes off on excursions for the World Bank, Noor is chief cook at home. Their daughters, Jehan and Zahara, especially like Noor's black-eyed peas. Noor admits that when Shirin is away he uses canned black-eyed peas.

Noorali's Black-Eyed Pea Curry

1 pound dried black-eyed peas
3 tablespoons butter or vegetable oil
2 medium onions, chopped
1 large green pepper, diced
2 cloves garlic, mashed
⅛ teaspoon cayenne
1 or 2 fresh hot chili peppers, halved and seeded
1 teaspoon turmeric
1 teaspoon curry powder
1 teaspoon ground coriander
2 fresh tomatoes, diced
1 cup heavy tomato puree
a few sprigs fresh coriander, chopped
1 tablespoon garamasala
juice of 1 small lime or 1 tablespoon lemon juice
salt

1. Cook black-eyed peas according to basic directions (see pages 23–26). Drain.

2. Heat butter and fry onions and green pepper until onions are golden brown.

3. Add garlic, cayenne, hot chilies, turmeric, curry powder, ground coriander and continue to fry and stir for 5 minutes.

4. Add tomatoes and puree. Cook another 5 minutes and add drained black-eyed peas and fresh coriander. Cook 10 minutes longer and add garamasala, lime or lemon juice, and salt. Serve immediately to 6 or 8.

This may be served with whole wheat pita bread or chapatis, rice, vegetables, Indian pickles, and yoghurt.

East Indians make paneer from cow or buffalo milk. It is similar to tofu (bean curd), made from soybean milk. Tofu is a good substitute in this delicious Indian dish.

Matar Paneer

(Peas and Cheese)

2 tablespoons peanut oil
1 tablespoon butter
2 squares (½ pound) pressed tofu (bean curd), diced
1 onion, chopped
1 large clove garlic, mashed
1 1-inch cube fresh ginger, peeled and finely minced
1 hot green chili pepper finely chopped
4 whole cloves
1 2-inch stick cinnamon, broken in half
6 whole cardamom pods
½ teaspoon turmeric
1 teaspoon ground coriander
2 cups peeled and chopped tomatoes (use fresh if possible)
3 cups fresh or frozen peas
½ cup water
salt
2 tablespoons chopped fresh coriander leaves

1. Heat peanut oil and butter in a large saucepan and fry diced bean curd until golden. Remove bean curd from pan with a slotted spoon and set aside.

193

2. To the remaining oil in the pan, add onion, garlic, ginger, chili, cloves, cinnamon stick, and cardamom pods. Fry until onion is soft but not browned.

3. Add turmeric and ground coriander and continue to fry 10 minutes, stirring constantly, so that spices will not burn.

4. Add tomatoes and bring to a boil. Reduce heat and cook another 10 minutes, stirring occasionally.

5. Add peas, water, salt, half the coriander leaves, and bean curd. Cook until peas are tender. Add more water if necessary. There should be a nice, thick gravy.

6. Pour into serving bowl and sprinkle remaining coriander leaves on top as garnish. Serve immediately with rice to 4.

Other Indian dishes, including dal, could be served with this.

Dals prepared in Pakistan differ from Indian preparations. Pakistani dal usually is thicker and dryer than Indian, and the flavoring is different.

Masoor dal is the very small and pretty salmon-colored dal. The color changes to golden when cooked.

Pakistani Masoor ki Dal

1 cup masoor dal
2 tablespoons butter
2 tablespoons oil
3 bay leaves
½ teaspoon whole cumin seeds
3 whole dried red peppers
¼ teaspoon turmeric
½ teaspoon cayenne (or to taste)
½ teaspoon ground ginger
2 large (or 3 medium) cloves garlic, mashed
1 rounded tablespoon tamarind extract or tamarind powder or the juice of 1 lemon

1. Cook dal according to basic directions (see pages 23–26), using 2½ cups water, until it disintegrates.

2. In skillet, melt butter and oil and brown bay leaves, cumin seeds, and peppers, being careful not to burn them.

3. Add to skillet, turmeric, cayenne, ginger, and garlic. Remove pan from heat when garlic is fragrant.

4. Shortly before serving, dissolve tamarind in dal. Then fry dal in the spices in the skillet until dal is nicely browned. Serves 4.

I enjoy rice or chapatis with dal, plus lots of yoghurt. A curried vegetable goes well, as does a light salad.

This dal recipe from Pakistan is simpler than most, but it has a delightful flavor.

Green Split Pea Dal

1 pound green split peas
2 tablespoons peanut oil
2 onions, chopped
1 clove garlic, mashed
1 tablespoon finely chopped fresh ginger
1 teaspoon turmeric
¼ teaspoon cayenne
1 teaspoon garamasala
½ cup tomato puree
a few sprigs fresh coriander leaves, chopped
salt

1. Cook split peas according to basic directions (see pages 23–26) until tender but not disintegrating.

2. Heat peanut oil in a saucepan and fry onions, garlic, and ginger until onions are transparent.

3. Add turmeric, cayenne, and garamasala. Cook, while stirring, for 3 or 4 minutes.

4. Add tomato puree and simmer mixture for 10 minutes, stirring occasionally.

5. Combine onion mixture in saucepan with split peas. Bring to a boil, reduce heat, and simmer 5 minutes or until thick and flavors have blended. Add coriander and salt. Cook 2 more minutes. Serves 6 to 8.

I like this dal served over brown rice and accompanied by yoghurt and a tossed salad.

A dish of channa dal and mustard greens is a tasty and nutritious treat. It is not surprising that this dish is so popular among Pakistanis.

Channa ki Dal and Mustard Greens

½ pound channa dal
1 pound mustard greens (or ½ pound frozen, chopped)
2 large cloves garlic, mashed
2 teaspoons ground ginger
½ teaspoon cayenne
2 teaspoons turmeric
4 tablespoons butter
salt

1. Cook dal according to basic directions (see pages 23–26) using 3 cups water.

2. Cook mustard greens in a minimum amount of water until tender.

3. Combine cooked dal with mustard greens, garlic, ginger, cayenne, and turmeric. Simmer 10 minutes uncovered.

4. Melt butter in a heated skillet. Add dal mixture and salt and brown for a few minutes. Stir occasionally.

5. Put dal and greens in a shallow baking dish and bake in a preheated 350°F. oven for about 10 minutes. Dal should be fairly dry. Serves 4.

Chapatis and rice go well with dal. Serve also with yoghurt and a tossed salad.

China

Japan

Polynesia

China, Japan, and Polynesia

These high-protein patties are delicious, and kids love them. If you cook them frequently, as I do, it is worthwhile cooking a large quantity of soybeans at one time and freezing them in batches of 2 cups.

Soybean-Rice Patties

1 cup dried soybeans (about 2 cups cooked)
4 cups cooked brown rice (2 cups dry)
1 large onion, chopped
1 large green pepper, chopped
1 clove garlic, mashed
2 tablespoons minced fresh ginger
1 tablespoon peanut oil
½ cup chopped water chestnuts
1 cup chopped fresh mushrooms
2 eggs
½ cup whole wheat flour
salt
¼ teaspoon white pepper
3 tablespoons tamari soy sauce
oil for frying

1. Cook soybeans until well done, according to basic directions (see pages 23–26). Drain and mash or put through a food grinder. They need not be thoroughly pureed.

2. Put cooked rice in a large mixing bowl. Add mashed soybeans.

3. Sauté onion, green pepper, garlic, and ginger in peanut oil until vegetables are lightly browned. Add them, along with water chestnuts and mushrooms, to the soybeans-rice.

4. With a fork or in a blender, mix together eggs and flour and add along with salt, pepper, and tamari.

5. Mix ingredients thoroughly.

6. Heat frying oil in a large skillet and drop in large spoonfuls (about ¼ cup) of soybean-rice mixture. Brown

on both sides. Serves 6 to 8. Pass hot mustard and tamari at the table.

I like to accompany the patties with stir-fried vegetables such as zucchini, Chinese cabbage, mushrooms, bean sprouts, and snow peas.

This is an adaptation of an unusually flavorful recipe that was circulated widely in Honolulu. Dick Morris and Don Raleigh, gourmet historians at the University of Hawaii, acquired the recipe and passed it on to me. Dick and Don will be surprised by the addition of doufu (the Chinese name for bean curd). I think it adds an interesting texture and nutritional quality.

Szechwan Eggplant with Doufu (Bean Curd)

3 medium (2 pounds) eggplants
½ cup peanut oil
4 cloves garlic, mashed
1 rounded tablespoon finely minced fresh ginger
4 tablespoons tamari soy sauce
1 tablespoon raw sugar
1 tablespoon rice or cider vinegar
¼ to ½ teaspoon cayenne
¾ pound firm doufu (bean curd), cut in ½-inch cubes

1. Cut eggplant into thumb-size pieces. Do not peel.

2. In a large skillet, fry eggplant in ½ cup less 1 tablespoon peanut oil, until soft. Remove and drain on paper towels.

3. Add remaining 1 tablespoon oil to skillet and sauté garlic and ginger for 1 minute. Add soy sauce, sugar, vinegar, and cayenne. Cook until the aroma drives you crazy.

4. Add doufu and eggplant. Mix gently. When it is all very hot, serve with brown rice to 4.

It is well known that Chinese stir-fried dishes are healthful and delicious. This one is no exception.

Doufu (Bean Curd) and Vegetable Stir-Fry

3 tablespoons tamari soy sauce
1 teaspoon liquid fructose sugar
¼ teaspoon ground ginger
1 clove garlic, mashed
3 tablespoons peanut oil
1 pound firm doufu (bean curd), cubed
1 large onion, sliced
2 cups thinly sliced celery
2 scallions, cut in 2-inch lengths
⅛ teaspoon crushed red pepper (optional)
½ pound mushrooms, sliced
4 cups sliced Chinese cabbage
½ pound bean sprouts
1 tablespoon cornstarch, dissolved in ¼ cup water

1. In a small bowl combine soy sauce, sugar, ginger, and garlic.

2. In a wok or large skillet, heat peanut oil until hot and fry cubes of doufu until they turn golden.

3. Drain doufu and put in the bowl with soy sauce mixture while frying vegetables. (Turn doufu cubes from time to time so that they all absorb some sauce.)

4. In the wok add onion, celery, scallions, and crushed red pepper to the remaining oil and stir-fry 3 minutes.

5. Add mushrooms and cook 2 minutes.

6. Add cabbage and cook 2 minutes.

7. Add bean sprouts, doufu cubes and sauce, and cornstarch mixture. Cover wok and cook until mixture boils and thickens. Serves 4.

Serve with rice and pass Korean kim chee as a condiment.

This hot and spicy dish is from Szechwan, a province in western China. It is said that a woman who lived there produced this dish for poor laborers for a very small fee. Ma means "numbing the tongue." Po refers to the woman's pock scars.

Ma Po's Doufu (Bean Curd)

1 pound pressed bean curd squares
6 dried Chinese mushrooms, soaked in 1 cup hot water
2 teaspoons salted black beans (optional)
2 tablespoons peanut oil
1 tablespoon sesame oil
1 green pepper, coarsely chopped
1 hot green pepper, finely chopped
2 cloves garlic, mashed
½ cup chopped green onions
2 tablespoons grated fresh ginger
2 tablespoons soy sauce
1 to 2 teaspoons hot chili paste
2 teaspoons cornstarch
1 teaspoon brown Szechwan peppercorn powder

1. Cut bean curd in ½-inch cubes and drop into boiling water. When the water returns to a boil, allow the cubes of bean curd to boil 1 minute. Drain and set them aside.

2. Rinse and soak mushrooms in 1 cup of hot water for 30 minutes. Drain, reserving the water. Remove and discard stems and chop mushrooms coarsely.

3. Soak black beans in water for 15 minutes. Drain and mash.

4. Heat combined oils in a wok or skillet. Add green and hot peppers, mushrooms, and garlic. Stir-fry until fragrant. Add green onions and ginger and cook 2 minutes.

5. Add black beans, soy sauce, hot chili paste, and ½ cup of the reserved mushroom soaking water. Continue to cook for 3 or 4 minutes.

6. Blend the cornstarch with 4 teaspoons of the mushroom soaking water and add to the mixture in the wok.

7. Add the bean curd and the peppercorn powder. Stir and cook until bean curd has partially absorbed the liquid and is heated through. Serves 6.

This should be eaten with plain rice. I like to accompany it with a combination of vegetables lightly stir-fried and seasoned with soy sauce. The vegetables may include Chinese cabbage, mushrooms, zucchini, bean sprouts, onions, and snow peas.

This preparation gets excellent ratings from my family and friends.

Stuffed Doufu (Bean Curd)

6 squares pressed doufu (about ½ inch thick)
2½ tablespoons peanut oil
Stuffing:
   ¼ cup coarsely chopped scallions
   ¼ cup coarsely chopped celery
   ¼ cup coarsely chopped green pepper
   ¼ cup coarsely chopped mushrooms
   ½ cup shredded Chinese cabbage
   ½ cup coarsely chopped mung bean sprouts
   1 egg, beaten
   1½ tablespoons soy sauce
   1 tablespoon cornstarch, dissolved in 1 tablespoon water
   ¼ teaspoon salt
   pinch cayenne
Sauce:
   1 cup vegetable broth
   1 tablespoon cornstarch, dissolved in 1 tablespoon water
   1 tablespoon soy sauce
   1 teaspoon finely chopped ginger
   1 clove garlic, mashed

1. Cut each bean curd square into 2 triangles. Then cut a slit along the long side to within ¼ inch of the other two sides to form a pocket. Cut pockets in all 12 bean curd triangles.

2. To make stuffing: In 1 tablespoon of the peanut oil, stir-fry scallions, celery, and green pepper for 3 minutes. Add mushrooms and cabbage and cook for 1 minute. Add bean sprouts and continue to stir-fry 1 minute longer.

3. Beat the egg and soy sauce together. Add dissolved cornstarch, salt, and cayenne. Pour the egg mixture over the frying vegetables and stir with chopsticks until every-

thing is well mixed and the egg is set. Remove from heat.

4. Stuff the doufu triangles with the vegetable filling.

5. In a heavy skillet, heat remaining oil. Sauté stuffed doufu triangles, on both sides, until they are lightly browned. Remove them from skillet as frying is completed and keep warm.

6. Now make the sauce: In the same skillet add vegetable broth, dissolved cornstarch, soy sauce, ginger, and garlic. Bring to a boil.

7. Add the fried bean curd triangles. Spoon some sauce over top, turn heat low, and cover. Simmer 10 minutes. Turn and cook another 10 minutes.

8. When cooked, remove triangles to a serving platter. Spoon sauce over stuffed doufu.

I like this following a soup and accompanied by steamed rice.

In Japan, cold tofu is a favorite food on hot summer days.

Tofu

slices of tofu (bean curd)
grated fresh ginger
chopped green onion
tamari soy sauce

1. Refrigerate tofu until very cold.
2. Slice and add the above toppings. Serve.

This was inspired by Honolulu, where sweet and sour foods abound.

Islander Soybeans

1 cup dried soybeans
2 tablespoons peanut oil
1 large onion, chopped
1 clove garlic, mashed
1 tablespoon finely minced fresh ginger
2 green peppers, cut in thin slices
1 cup sliced celery
2 cups sliced Chinese cabbage
2 cups bean sprouts
½ cup bamboo shoots, cut into matchsticks
1 1-pound can unsweetened pineapple chunks
1 tablespoon cornstarch
¼ cup soy sauce
2 tablespoons rice vinegar
dash cayenne
1 fresh tomato, cut in wedges

1. Cook soybeans according to basic directions (see pages 23–26). Drain.

2. In a large wok or frying pan, heat peanut oil and fry onion, garlic, and ginger for about 3 minutes. Add green peppers and celery and stir-fry another 2 minutes. Add cabbage, bean sprouts, bamboo shoots, and soybeans, and continue to stir-fry another minute.

3. Drain pineapple and dissolve cornstarch in the pineapple juice. To the wok, add pineapple, cornstarch-juice mixture, and remaining ingredients, except tomato.

4. Cook until mixture boils for 1 minute. Garnish with tomato wedges and serve directly from the wok with brown rice. Serves 5 or 6.

This exotic pilau can be served as a main or side dish, and it travels well to picnics and pot luck suppers.

Polynesian Pilau

¾ cup dried black-eyed peas
2 cups brown rice
4 tablespoons butter
1 cup raw cashews
1 large onion, chopped
1 1-inch cube fresh ginger, peeled and finely chopped
1 large green pepper, diced
4 cups sliced celery
1 carrot, scraped and sliced in thin discs
1 cup green peas
1 cup pineapple tidbits (fresh is better)
2 tablespoons pineapple juice
2 tablespoons soy sauce
salt
dash hot pepper sauce

1. Cook black-eyed peas according to basic directions (see pages 23–26). Drain.

2. Cook brown rice in double its volume of lightly salted water until rice is tender and fluffy.

3. In a large, heavy skillet, melt 1 tablespoon of the butter and lightly brown the cashews. Remove cashews and reserve.

4. Add onion, ginger, and another tablespoon of the butter to skillet and cook on medium heat until onion is soft. Add green pepper, celery, and remaining butter. Stir-fry vegetables until celery is tender-crisp.

5. Cook carrot separately, in a little water, until tender. Drain.

6. To the vegetables in the skillet, add peas, pineapple, pineapple juice, soy sauce, salt, and pepper sauce. Bring to a boil and allow to boil for 1 minute. Add black-eyed peas and carrots. Bring to boil again and remove from heat.

7. Combine vegetable mixture with rice and adjust seasonings. Place on serving platter and sprinkle cashews evenly over top. Serves 4 to 8. You may pass additional soy sauce at the table.

Africa

I call this safari beans because it was while on safari in Kenya that we had this wonderful repast. Our Kenyan friends prepared this dish from canned beans, out in the bush over an open fire in a collapsible tin oven. Later, when I recreated the recipe in my own kitchen in Syracuse, New York, I was really pleased to find that it tasted almost as good.

Safari Beans

1 pound dried great northern beans
1 large onion, chopped
2 tablespoons butter
salt
white pepper
3 or 4 tomatoes, peeled and sliced
1½ cups grated cheddar cheese

1. Cook beans according to basic directions (see pages 23–26). Drain.

2. Butter a deep, 3-quart casserole dish.

3. In a large skillet, sauté onion in butter until thoroughly cooked but not browned. Combine with drained beans, salt, and pepper.

4. Place ⅓ of the beans and onions in casserole dish. Cover with a layer of sliced tomatoes. Salt and pepper tomatoes lightly. Sprinkle ⅓ of the cheese over the tomatoes.

5. Repeat these layers twice.

6. Cover dish and bake at 350°F. for 25 minutes. Remove cover and bake another 5 minutes. Serves 6 to 8.

Homemade bran muffins and a large mixed vegetable salad are pleasant additions to this casserole.

Mataha, a Kikuyu dish, is an old staple in East Africa. It is highly nutritious and the ingredients are grown in the shambas *(gardens) in the villages. The flavorful soup sometimes served with it is a more recent addition.*

Nyambura Mwangi, from Nakuru, Kenya, who shared her recipe with me, says that the amount of beans in the dish depends on the wealth of the family. White maize (field corn), as the least expensive food, is used more abundantly. This recipe calls for spinach, but Africans would more likely use tender pumpkin leaves.

Mataha

1 pound dried beans (any variety will do)
1 15-ounce can whole hominy
5 or 6 (2 pounds) potatoes, peeled and cut in pieces
10 ounces spinach or other greens
¼ pound butter
salt

1. Cook beans according to basic directions (see pages 23–26). Drain.

2. Cook hominy until very soft. Drain.

3. Boil potatoes, drain and set aside.

4. Cook spinach in just the water clinging to its leaves after washing. Drain.

5. Combine all ingredients in a large saucepan and mash (not thoroughly) with a potato masher. The mataha should be fairly dry and stiff.

6. Place pan over low heat and cook slowly until heated throughout. Serves 6 to 8.

Mataha may be eaten as is, but I prefer it with the special soup that usually accompanies it.

Vegetable Soup for Mataha

1 onion, chopped
1 clove garlic, mashed
1 tablespoon curry powder
2 tablespoons peanut oil
1 15-ounce can tomatoes, chopped
6 cups water
3½ cups chopped cabbage
3½ cups cauliflower, cut in small flowerettes
2 cups fresh spinach, cut in pieces
1 cup fresh or frozen peas
salt

1. In a large soup kettle, sauté onion, garlic, and curry powder in peanut oil until onion is soft but not brown.

2. Add tomatoes and cook, stirring occasionally, for 5 minutes.

3. Add water, cabbage, and cauliflower. Bring to a boil, reduce heat, and cook 5 minutes.

4. Add spinach and peas. Cook until all vegetables are tender. Add salt.

Place a large spoonful of mataha in a soup plate. Pour soup and vegetables over and serve.

The fava bean is also called the broad bean, Windsor bean, and horse bean. It is little used in the United States but has been the principal bean of Europe. The large-seeded type originated in the Mediterranean region, and the small-seeded variety in the Middle East. It is an important food in North Africa, including the Sudan.

Sudanese Fava Beans

½ pound dried and skinned fava beans
2 tablespoons peanut oil
1 onion, chopped
1 clove garlic, crushed
4 whole cloves
1 2-inch stick cinnamon, broken in half
1 teaspoon ground cumin
¾ teaspoon ground cinnamon
⅛ teaspoon cayenne
1 or 2 whole green chili peppers, quartered
1 cup chopped tomatoes
1 8-ounce can tomato sauce
salt
6 small hard-cooked eggs (make some cuts in them, attractively, with
  a knife)

1. Cook fava beans until soft according to basic directions (see pages 23–26). Drain and reserve broth.

2. In a large heavy skillet, heat peanut oil and sauté onion, garlic, cloves, and stick cinnamon until onion is transparent.

3. Add ground cumin, ground cinnamon, cayenne, and pieces of chilies. Continue to sauté, stirring constantly, until mixture is lightly browned.

4. Add tomatoes, tomato sauce, and enough bean broth to make a thickish gravy. Cook for 15 minutes.

5. Add beans, salt, and eggs and cook 5 to 10 minutes to heat the beans and eggs thoroughly and to allow flavors to blend. Serves 4 to 6.

This may be served with brown rice, bulgur, or pita bread. A tossed salad makes a pleasant accompaniment.

I found that this North African dish usually made with meat is just as tasty and nutritious without it.

Couscous Tunisienne

¾ pound dried chick-peas
2 large onions, chopped
2 large cloves garlic, mashed
4 tablespoons butter
2 tablespoons olive oil
1 2-inch stick cinnamon, broken in half
¼ teaspoon allspice
½ teaspoon turmeric
1 teaspoon ground coriander
1 1-pound can tomatoes, chopped
1 vegetable bouillon cube
6 carrots, scraped and cut in discs
1 large green pepper, cut in large cubes
2 medium zucchini, halved lengthwise, then sliced
salt
¼ teaspoon cayenne
1 tablespoon lemon juice
1 pound couscous

1. Cook chick-peas according to basic directions (see pages 23–26), increase water to 10 cups. Drain and reserve broth.

2. Sauté onions and garlic in 2 tablespoons of the butter and olive oil until onions are transparent. Add spices and continue to cook until onions are lightly browned.

3. Add tomatoes, 6 cups chick-pea broth (add water if necessary), bouillon cube, carrots, green pepper, and zucchini. Cook until the vegetables are half done.

4. Add chick-peas, salt, cayenne, and lemon juice. Bring to a boil, reduce heat, and simmer while couscous steams for 20 minutes.

5. To cook couscous, follow directions on package or spread couscous in a large shallow pan and stir in 8 cups cold water. Drain through a strainer, return to pan, and let stand about 20 minutes. Occasionally fluff up couscous with a fork or fingers to keep grains separated. Line a steamer, colander, or couscousier with cheesecloth. Gradually add couscous, rubbing it between the fingers.

Steam over water, uncovered, about 20 minutes. Remove from water, fluff it again, and steam over vegetables and broth 20 minutes. Place couscous in a bowl and add remaining 2 tablespoons butter.

6. Serve couscous in individual bowls with some chickpeas, vegetables, and broth over, or put couscous in the center of a large serving bowl and spoon chick-peas, vegetables, and some of the broth around it. Pass remaining broth at the table. Serves 6 to 8.

A pleasing dessert would be custard and stewed, dried fruits.

In Nigeria, these tasty morsels are often taken with breakfast. They also are eaten as a snack or as part of a meal.

Akara

(West African Black-Eyed Pea Fritters)

½ pound dried black-eyed peas
1 onion, coarsely chopped
2 tomatoes, quartered
2 to 4 tablespoons water
salt
½ to 1 teaspoon cayenne
peanut oil for deep-frying

1. Place the black-eyed peas in a deep bowl. Cover with triple their volume of warm water and let them soak overnight or for several hours.

2. Drain the peas, add hot water and let them soak for 5 minutes. Rub the peas vigorously between the palms of hands to loosen and remove their skins. As the skins float to the surface of the water, skim them off with a strainer.

3. Drain the peas and add more hot water. Let them soak about 5 minutes. Again, rub the peas between hands and skim off the skins from the water.

4. Repeat this process until all the black-eyed peas are skinned. It helps, in getting the last few peas skinned, to rub them between towels and to go over them with a

rolling pin. Some of the beans will crack and skins will loosen. Put them in warm water again and skim off the skins.

5. Drain the skinned peas and place about ½ of them, ½ of the onion, ½ of the tomatoes and 1 to 2 tablespoons water in a blender jar. Blend at high speed for 30 seconds. Scrape down sides of jar and blend until fairly smooth. Pour contents into a bowl.

6. Blend remaining peas, onion, tomatoes, and 1 to 2 tablespoons water and pour into the bowl.

7. Combine black-eyed pea puree with salt and cayenne.

8. Drop the mixture by tablespooons into deep oil heated to 350°F. Fry a few at a time, turning them frequently, until lightly browned on all sides and cooked throughout. If fritters do not hold together when frying, place puree in a strainer to remove some of the moisture.

9. Drain on paper towels and serve hot.

This delicately flavored specialty of West Africa was prepared for us by Ebikake Yeri-Obidake, Prince of Oproza in the Niger River delta of Nigeria. Prince Yeri-Obidake says that people are enthusiastic about attending functions when they know that moin-moin will be served. It is frequently prepared for special occasions.

Moin-moin can be baked in a shallow baking dish with a tight-fitting lid or it can be steamed. In the Prince's home, it is wrapped in large leaves for steaming. It can also be wrapped in aluminum foil if the foil is first oiled.

Moin-moin can be cut in about 2-inch diamond or rectangular shapes and served with the main meal, or it can enhance a buffet table.

Moin-Moin

(Nigerian Black-Eyed Pea Mousse)

1⅔ cup dried black-eyed peas
2 onions, coarsely chopped
4 tomatoes, quartered
⅓ cup water
¼ cup red palm oil (use all peanut oil if palm oil is unavailable)
¼ cup peanut oil
salt
½ to 1 teaspooon cayenne
4 hard-cooked eggs, peeled and quartered

1. Place the peas in a deep bowl and pour in triple their volume of hot water. Let them soak overnight or for several hours.

2. Drain the peas, add hot water and let them soak for about 5 minutes. Rub the peas vigorously between the palms of the hands to loosen and remove their skins. As the skins float to the surface of the water, skim them off with a strainer.

3. Drain the peas and add more hot water. Let them soak about 5 minutes. Again, rub the peas between hands and skim the skins off the water.

4. Repeat the process until all the black-eyed peas are skinned. It helps, in getting the last few peas skinned, to rub them between towels and to go over them with a

rolling pin. Some of the beans will crack and skins will loosen. Put them in warm water again and skim off the skins.

5. Drain the skinned peas and place about ⅓ of them, ⅓ of the onions, ⅓ of the tomatoes, ⅓ of the water, and ⅓ of the oils in a blender jar. Blend at high speed for 30 seconds. Scrape down the sides of the jar and blend until mixture is smooth. Pour puree into a bowl.

6. Blend another ⅓ of the peas, onions, tomatoes, water, and oils until smooth. Pour into the bowl.

7. Puree the remaining ⅓ of the ingredients and pour into the bowl. Combine salt and cayenne with puree.

8. Stir in eggs. (Sometimes a few sardines or a little tuna is used instead of the eggs.)

9. Pour into an oiled, shallow baking dish. Tightly cover and bake in a 300°F. oven for 1 hour. Cut into diamond or rectangular shapes and serve from baking dish or platter.

10. Moin-moin can be spooned onto oiled aluminum foil rectangles, sealed, and placed on a rack over boiling water or in a steamer for 1 hour.

Middle East

Middle East

Among the most welcome additions to the American scene are the numerous Middle Eastern restaurants which have brought a new and exciting cuisine to many American cities. A few years ago these restaurants were confined to four or five of our largest cities. Falafel, which are quickly becoming as popular as hamburgers, can easily be made at home.

Falafel

(Deep Fried Chick-Pea Cakes)

½ pound dried chick-peas
3 cups water
1 onion, chopped
2 cloves garlic, finely minced
½ cup chopped parsley
1 small hot chili pepper, seeded and chopped
½ teaspoon ground cumin
salt
¾ teaspoon baking powder
oil for deep-frying

1. Place rinsed chick-peas in a saucepan with water. Bring to a rolling boil and let boil for 2 minutes. Cover pan, remove from heat, and let stand 2 hours or longer. Drain well.

2. Combine drained chick-peas, onion, garlic, parsley, hot pepper, cumin, salt, and baking powder. Put through a food grinder twice.

3. Refrigerate until ready for hot falafel. (Mixture may be frozen, but baking powder should be added only after it thaws.)

4. When ready to fry, shape into firm patties 2 inches in diameter and ½ inch thick.

5. Drop a few at a time into deep, hot oil until brown and cooked through. Carefully turn them once or twice. Drain on paper towels.

6. Cut in half warmed, whole wheat, Arabic pita bread. Open the pocket and put in about 2 falafel. Add chopped onion, chopped tomato, and chopped cucumber. Top with tarator or tahini sauce. Eat immediately. Makes more than 1 dozen falafel.

Tarator or Tahini Sauce

½ cup tahini (sesame seed paste)
juice of 1½ lemons
1 clove garlic, mashed
salt
3 to 4 tablespoons water

Combine tahini, lemon juice, garlic, and salt. Add just enough water to make a thick sauce. Beat until smooth.

Simple to prepare and delightful to eat!

Lebanese Spinach and Chick-Peas

¾ cup dried chick-peas
2 pounds fresh spinach
¼ cup olive oil
1 large onion, chopped
⅛ teaspoon allspice
⅛ teaspoon white pepper
salt
2 tablespoons lemon juice

1. Cook chick-peas according to basic directions (see pages 23–26). Drain and reserve broth.
2. Wash spinach and cook with just the water clinging to it until spinach wilts. Drain and set spinach aside.
3. Heat olive oil and cook onion until well cooked and lightly browned. Add chick-peas, spinach, and remaining ingredients. Cook 5 minutes to allow flavors to blend. Serves 6.

Serve with whole wheat pita bread or brown rice.

Black-eyed peas are prepared by people around the world because of their nutritional value and their excellent flavor. This is yet another delicious rendition.

Syrian Black-Eyed Peas

½ pound dried black-eyed peas
⅓ cup olive oil
1 large onion, chopped
3 cloves garlic, mashed
1 small hot green pepper, minced
1 28-ounce can plum tomatoes, undrained and chopped
1 tablespoon chopped fresh parsley
salt

1. Cook peas according to basic directions (see pages 23–26). Drain, reserving ½ cup of the broth.
2. In a large saucepan, heat olive oil and brown onion, garlic, and hot pepper. Add tomatoes and reserved pea broth. Cook 10 minutes.
3. Add black-eyed peas, parsley, and salt. Cook an additional 10 minutes or until flavors have blended and vegetables are thoroughly cooked. Serves 3 or 4.

This goes well over bulgur or brown rice.

Mujaddara, which means "nails of the knees" is so named because of its nutritional richness. It is thought that farmers especially need this to give them the strength to carry out their hard work. This so called poor man's food is highly prized in the Middle East, especially in Lebanon, Palestine, and Jordan.

Mujaddara

(Lentils and Rice)

½ pound lentils
¾ cup brown rice
3 medium-large onions
⅓ cup olive oil
1 teaspoon ground cumin
salt
¼ teaspoon white pepper

1. Cook lentils according to basic directions (see pages 23–26), until tender, using 4 cups water. Drain, reserving broth for cooking rice.

2. Cook rice in 2 cups of lightly salted lentil broth until tender. If there are not 2 cups of broth, make up the difference with water. Set aside cooked rice.

3. Slice 2 of the onions; set aside the outer rings for garnish and chop the inner part of the onions. Chop the third onion.

4. In a large saucepan, heat olive oil and fry onion rings until brown. Remove from pan and reserve for garnish.

5. Fry chopped onion in the same pan until lightly browned. Add cumin and continue cooking over low heat until onions are very soft.

6. Combine lentils, rice, and cooked onions with the oil. Cook over low heat for 15 to 20 minutes, stirring occasionally. Add salt and pepper and mix well.

7. Pour onto a platter and garnish with reserved onion rings. Serve warm or at room temperature. Serves 4.

A salad always accompanies mujaddara. It usually consists of romaine lettuce, tomatoes, cucumbers, and a lemon juice and olive oil dressing.

Laban bi khyar (yoghurt and cucumber) is frequently served too. Slice cold cucumbers and add them to yoghurt with a little salt and dried or fresh mint leaves. In summer, ice cubes are sometimes added.

In Egypt, ful mudamas is the national dish. My friend Mona El Bayadi Racine shared her recipe. She says that it is eaten for breakfast, lunch, or dinner, or anytime one is hungry.

Egyptian Ful Mudamas

1 pound small fava beans
2 cloves garlic, mashed
2 teaspoons ground cumin
2 to 4 tablespoons lemon juice
½ cup olive oil
salt
⅛ teaspoon cayenne

1. Cook beans according to basic directions (see pages 23–26). I recommend using a pressure cooker or else buying dried beans that have had the skins removed. The skinless beans take little time to cook. Canned fava beans may be used. I rinse them before cooking for better digestibility.

2. The cooked beans can be mashed, left whole, or some of them can be mashed. If mashed, the finished product should be the consistency of a thick gravy.

3. Add garlic, cumin, lemon juice, olive oil, salt, and cayenne.

4. Serve warm or at room temperature. Serves 6 to 8.

Ful mudamas are always eaten with pita bread and often with sliced fresh vegetables (onions, cucumbers, tomatoes, and green peppers) as well. At breakfast, they are sometimes eaten with soft-boiled eggs.

Desserts

Desserts

This unique pie gets high ratings from all who have savored it. The filling is not overly sweet or rich and goes exceptionally well with the whole wheat pie crust.

White Bean Pie with Almonds

⅔ cup dried baby lima beans
1 cup milk
1 cup heavy cream
½ cup liquid fructose sugar
4 eggs
2 teaspoons vanilla
¼ teaspoon salt
1 10-inch unbaked whole wheat pastry shell
nutmeg
toasted sliced almonds

1. Cook beans according to basic directions (see pages 23–26). Drain well.

2. Place drained beans, milk, cream, sugar, eggs, vanilla, and salt in a blender jar. Blend until smooth. Or mash beans and beat with other ingredients in a bowl.

3. Pour into an unbaked pie shell and sprinkle with nutmeg. Bake in a preheated 350°F. oven for 60 to 70 minutes or until an inserted knife emerges clean.

4. Cool and sprinkle with almonds before serving.

Our son Robert loves bean pies but cannot decide which one he prefers. I think this is a very good one.

Pinto Pie

⅔ cup dried pinto beans
¼ cup liquid fructose sugar
½ cup pure maple syrup
¼ cup orange juice
½ teaspoon grated orange rind
1 tablespoon lemon juice
3 eggs
dash salt
1 teaspoon cinnamon
½ teaspoon ginger
¼ teaspoon cloves
¼ teaspoon nutmeg
1 13-ounce can evaporated milk
1 10-inch, deep dish pie shell (recipe follows)

1. Cook beans according to basic directions (see pages 23–26). Drain and mash.

2. Place in blender, beans, fructose, maple syrup, orange juice and rind, lemon juice, eggs, salt, and spices. Blend at high speed until everything is well blended. Stir in milk.

3. Pour into prepared pie shell and bake in a preheated 350°F. oven for about 1 hour or until an inserted knife emerges clean. Serve cool or cold with whipped cream, if desired.

Makes 1 large shell, for a 10- to 12-inch pie.

Whole Wheat Pie Crust

1 cup whole wheat pastry flour
⅓ cup unbleached white flour
½ teaspoon salt
½ cup butter
3 tablespoons cold water

1. Combine both flours and salt in a mixing bowl.

2. Cut the butter into the flour, using a pastry blender or 2 knives, until the mixture resembles coarse cornmeal.

3. Sprinkle water evenly over mixture. Toss well with a fork, to allow moisture to spread, and gather into a ball.

4. Roll out, between sheets of plastic wrap, from the center out in all directions, until evenly rolled about ⅛ inch thick. The dough should be about 1 inch larger than an inverted pie pan. (For a deep dish pie the dough should be 1½ inches larger than the pie pan.)

5. Carefully pull off plastic sheets and roll dough loosely over rolling pin. Lift it into ungreased pie pan and ease it into place without stretching it.

6. Trim edge of the pastry, leaving about ½ inch overhang. Turn pastry under all the way around the rim of the pan. Make a fluted edge with the fingers.

7. Fill the pie and bake according to pie recipe directions.

This produces about seven pounds of delicious holiday fare.

Fruitcake

⅔ cup dried baby lima beans or any kind of beans on hand (1 cup
  mashed)
1½ cups pitted dates, sliced
1 cup dried figs, coarsely chopped
1¼ cup dried apricots, coarsely chopped
⅔ cup seedless raisins
⅔ cup golden raisins
1½ cups thinly sliced Brazil nuts
1½ cups coarsely chopped walnuts
2 cups whole wheat pastry flour
2 cups date sugar
1 tablespoon baking powder
½ teaspoon salt
1 teaspoon cinnamon
½ teaspoon ginger
¼ teaspoon nutmeg
⅛ teaspoon cloves
5 large eggs
½ cup skim milk
½ cup melted butter
½ cup peanut oil
2 tablespoons blackstrap molasses
grated rind and juice of 1 lemon
1 teaspoon vanilla
½ cup orange juice
½ cup honey

1. Cook beans according to basic directions (see pages 23–26). Drain and mash.

2. Prepare fruits and nuts, combine with 3 tablespoons of the flour, and set aside.

3. Line 2 greased 9 × 5 × 3-inch loaf pans with brown or waxed paper and grease the paper.

4. Preheat oven to 300°F.

5. Combine in a large mixing bowl, remaining flour, sugar, baking powder, salt, cinnamon, ginger, nutmeg, and cloves.

6. Make a well in dry ingredients and add eggs, milk, butter, oil, and molasses. Mix thoroughly.

7. Stir in lemon juice and rind and vanilla.

8. Mix fruits and nuts into batter.

9. Divide the batter equally between the 2 pans. Place a large, shallow baking pan of hot water on lower shelf in oven to prevent cakes from drying, and place cakes in the middle of the oven.

10. Bake about 1½ hours or until a toothpick inserted in center of cake emerges clean.

11. Bring to a boil orange juice and honey, and pour over the cakes. Pierce some holes in the tops of the cakes so that the liquid seeps through.

12. When cakes are cool, remove from pans, peel off paper, and wrap in plastic wrap. They will keep in the refrigerator for up to 3 weeks. They may also be frozen.

To be correct, eight kinds of fruits and nuts should be used in this pudding because they are the "treasures." No one minds, however, finding more treasures, should you wish to use them.

Eight Treasure Pudding

butter
mixture of Western or Chinese dried and preserved fruits and nuts
1½ cups uncooked glutinous rice (mochi rice)
1½ cups water
2 tablespoons peanut oil
2 tablespoons natural sugar
sweet red bean paste (see recipe page 228)

1. Butter a deep bowl or mold (about 6 inches in diameter) and arrange fruits and nuts on bottom and up sides in an attractive pattern.

2. Rinse rice, drain it, and put in pan with 1½ cups water. Bring to a boil and cook and stir for 5 minutes or until water is absorbed. Reduce heat to very low, put a lid on the pan, and cook an additional 15 minutes. Add oil and sugar to rice and mix well.

3. Place ⅔ of the rice in the bowl, uniformly covering the fruits and nuts on the bottom and up the sides of the bowl, forming a shell.

4. Put bean paste in the center of the rice, ½ inch from

the top, and cover the bean paste with the remaining rice, pressing it down. The bean paste should be totally enclosed in the center of the pudding.

5. Place the bowl, uncovered, in a steamer and steam for 2 hours.

6. Invert bowl to unmold, and serve hot with lemon sauce.

Lemon Sauce

1 cup water
2 tablespoons liquid fructose sugar
1 tablespoon cornstarch, dissolved in 1 tablespoon cold water
2 teaspoons lemon juice (or to taste)

1. Bring water and fructose to a boil.

2. Blend dissolved cornstarch into water and fructose mixture.

3. Add lemon juice and cook until thickened. Serve over the pudding.

This delicious bean filling can be used in cakes, pastries, cookies, or in any dessert where a filling is required.

Sweet Red Bean Paste

½ pound dried adzuki beans (Oriental red beans)
⅔ cup natural sugar, or more according to taste
2 tablespoons butter
2 tablespoons peanut oil

1. Cook beans according to basic directions (see pages 23–26). Drain beans and reserve broth.

2. Puree beans in blender, in batches, using a very small amount of bean broth to facilitate the process.

3. Heat a wok or large skillet and cook and stir the puree until mixture is very thick.

4. Add sugar and continue cooking and stirring until sugar is dissolved.

228

5. Gradually add butter and finally oil, incorporating each into the mixture. The mixture should resemble a fudge icing.

This is a basic filling used in Chinese and Japanese pastries and desserts, but it may be used in Western desserts as well. It is sold in cans and found in specialty foods stores where Oriental foods are sold. The Chinese name is *dow sa* and the Japanese name is *an*.

The adaptable sweetened bean paste goes very well in this American pastry.

Sweet Bean-Filled Pastries

Pastry:
  ½ cup butter
  3 ounces cream cheese
  ½ cup whole wheat flour
  ½ cup unbleached white flour
  ¼ teaspoon salt
Filling:
  ¾ cup sweet red bean paste (see recipe page 228)
  ½ cup chopped walnuts
  ½ teaspoon vanilla
1 egg, beaten (thinned with water)

1. Allow butter and cream cheese to soften at room temperature; blend.

2. Combine flours and salt and cut into cream cheese mixture with a pastry blender or 2 knives.

3. Gather dough in a ball, divide in 2 parts, wrap in plastic wrap and chill 30 minutes.

4. Roll out dough as you would for pie crust, about ⅛ inch thick. Cut the dough into rounds with a 3-inch cutter.

5. Place in the center of each round 1 teaspoon of filling. Fold over rounds and crimp edges. Continue rolling, cutting out, and filling pastries until all dough has been used.

6. Place filled pastries on a baking sheet and brush on top of each some beaten egg thinned with a little water. Bake at 425°F. for about 10 minutes or until lightly browned. Makes about 24 pastries.

The versatile, sweetened red bean paste is used throughout East Asia, including the Philippines. My dear friend from the Philippines, Flo Lewis, has served us halo-halo (which means mix-mix) in various combinations. It is easy to prepare, attractive, and a refreshing and delicious dessert.

Halo-Halo

fresh, frozen, or canned fruits of your choice (cantaloupe is especially
    good) and/or Philippine preserves such as macapuno (young
    sweetened coconut sport), sweet kaong (sugar palm), and sweet
    langka (jackfruit).
crushed ice
sweetened red bean paste
half and half, cream, or evaporated milk (Flo prefers evaporated milk,
    while my preference is half and half or cream)

1. Layer fruits and/or preserves in stemmed glasses using about 1 tablespoon of each. The preserves are very sweet so use them sparingly.

2. Add several spoons of crushed ice.

3. Top with a rounded tablespoon of sweetened bean paste.

4. Pass a pitcher of half and half, cream, or evaporated milk. Pour, mix, and enjoy.

I cannot resist adding this recipe for bean popsicles. They really are very good.

In Hawaii, there are many refreshment stands offering "Shave Ice"—they sell cups of shaved ice with sweetened red bean paste or colorful syrups poured over. These bean popsicles remind me of "Shave Ice."

Sweetened Red Bean Paste Popsicles

sweetened red bean paste (see recipe page 228)
water

1. Mix equal parts of bean paste and water.
2. Freeze in ice cube trays. Before popsicles are fully frozen, insert wooden picks.

These muffins are chock full of vitamins, protein, and fiber, and are delicious too. They are almost a complete food in themselves.

Apple Bran Muffins

½ cup dried baby lima beans
1 cup whole wheat flour
1 cup bran or 100% bran cereal
1 teaspoon baking powder
½ teaspoon baking soda
¼ teaspoon salt
¼ teaspoon cinnamon
pinch nutmeg
½ cup walnuts, chopped
1 apple, peeled and grated
½ cup raisins
1 egg, beaten
¾ cup milk
⅓ cup honey
3 tablespoons peanut oil

231

1. Cook beans according to basic directions (see pages 23–26). Drain, mash, and set aside.
2. Combine dry ingredients with nuts and fruits.
3. Add, all at once, mashed beans, egg, milk, honey, and oil.
4. Stir quickly and only enough to blend.
5. Immediately spoon into well-greased muffin tins. Fill the cups about ⅔ full.
6. Bake in preheated oven at 375°F. for 25 to 30 minutes.
7. Serve immediately. If serving later, remove them from tins and place on rack to cool.
8. To warm muffins, wrap in aluminum foil or place in a paper bag. Place in 400°F. oven for about 5 minutes.

The addition of cooked beans to this delicious and nutritious sweet bread provides a high protein content and produces a moist and fine-textured bread.

I prefer using cooked beans to soybean flour, which is frequently used in baked goods, because soybean flour can leave an unpleasant taste.

I choose to use baby limas because they have a delicate flavor and smooth texture, and they cook very quickly. One can even eliminate the soaking if in a hurry. Other cooked or canned beans can be used, if they are on hand, with excellent results.

Cranberry Bean Bread

⅔ cup dried baby lima beans (1 cup mashed)
1¾ cup whole wheat pastry flour
1 tablespoon baking powder
1 teaspoon salt
1 teaspoon cinnamon
¼ teaspoon nutmeg
1¾ cups date sugar
1 cup chopped walnuts
½ cup peanut oil
2 eggs, slightly beaten
½ cup skim milk
1 teaspoon vanilla
2 cups (½ pound) cranberries (if frozen, do not thaw)

1. Cook beans according to basic directions (see pages 23–26). Drain and mash. Make 1 cup of bean puree and set aside.

2. Preheat oven to 350°F.

3. Grease 2 8 × 4-inch loaf pans.

4. Measure into a large bowl, flour, baking powder, salt, cinnamon, nutmeg, sugar, and nuts. Mix thoroughly and make a well in the center.

5. Add the beans, oil, eggs, milk, and vanilla. Mix well and stir in the cranberries. The batter will be stiff.

6. Pour batter into the loaf pans. Bake for 1 hour or until a toothpick inserted in the center of the bread emerges clean. It may be red if you pick through a cranberry.

A slice of this healthful and delicious bread is a satisfying breakfast, but can be enjoyed at any time.

Banana Bran Bread

⅔ cup dried baby lima beans (1 cup mashed)
1¾ cups whole wheat pastry flour
1 cup bran or 100% bran cereal
2 teaspoons baking powder
½ teaspoon baking soda
½ teaspoon salt
1 cup chopped nuts
1½ cups (2 or 3) mashed bananas
3 tablespoons peanut oil
⅓ cup honey
2 eggs
1 teaspoon vanilla

1. Cook beans according to basic directions (see pages 23–26). Drain and mash.

2. Mix dry ingredients and combine with mashed beans, mashed bananas, oil, honey, eggs, and vanilla. Stir only enough to blend.

3. Pour into a well-greased 5 × 9 × 3-inch loaf pan and bake in a preheated 350°F. oven 60 to 70 minutes or until a toothpick inserted in the bread emerges clean and the top is golden brown.

4. After 5 minutes, remove from pan and cool on a rack.

List of Recipes

Hors d'oeuvres

Soups

Salads

Main Dishes

United States of America

Europe

Latin America

237